The Evaluation of Educational Programmes: Methods, Uses and Benefits

EUROPEAN MEETINGS ON EDUCATIONAL RESEARCH

Part A
Reports of educational research symposia, colloquies, and workshops organised under the auspices of the Council of Europe

Part B
European conferences of directors of educational research institutions organised in cooperation with UNESCO, the UNESCO Institute for Education in Hamburg, and the Council of Europe

Part A: Volume 24

COUNCIL OF EUROPE — STRASBOURG
THE SCOTTISH COUNCIL FOR RESEARCH IN EDUCATION

The Evaluation of Educational Programmes: Methods, Uses and Benefits

REPORT OF THE EDUCATIONAL RESEARCH WORKSHOP
HELD IN NORTH BERWICK (SCOTLAND)
22-25 NOVEMBER 1988

EDITED BY

The Scottish Council for Research in Education

SWETS & ZEITLINGER B.V. AMSTERDAM / LISSE   1990

SWETS & ZEITLINGER INC. ROCKLAND, MA / BERWYN, PA   *PUBLISHING SERVICE*

Library of Congress Cataloging-in-Publication Data

Educational Research Workshop (1988 : North Berwick, Scotland)
      The evaluation of educational programmes : methods, uses, and benefits : report of the Educational Research Workshop held in North Berwick, Scotland, 22-25 November 1988 / edited by the Scottish Council for Research in Education.
      168 p. 16x24 cm. — (European Meetings on Educational Research. Part A : v. 24)
      At head of title: Council of Europe—Strasbourg.
      Includes bibliographical references.
      ISBN 9026510268
      1. Educational evaluation—Congresses. I. Scottish Council for Research in Education. II. Council of Europe. III. Title. IV. Series.
LB2822.75.E33   1988
370'.7'8—dc20   90-30879
                                                                                                                    CIP

CIP-gegevens Koninklijke Bibliotheek, Den Haag

Evaluation

The evaluation of educational programmes: methods, uses and benefits : report of the educational research workshop held in North Berwick (Scotland), 22-25 November, 1988 / ed. by the Scottish Council for Research in Education. - Amsterdam [etc.] : Swets & Zeitlinger. - (European meetings on educational research. ISSN 0924-0578 ; vol. 24, pt A)
Met lit. opg.
ISBN 90-265-1026-8 geb.
SISI eu 452.2 UDC 371.012(4) NUGI 724
Trefw.: onderwijs ; Europa ; onderzoek.

Printed in the Netherlands by Offsetdrukkerij Kanters B.V., Alblasserdam

All rights reserved.
No part of this publication may be reproduced, stored in a retrieval system, or transmitted, in any form or by any means, electronic, mechanical, photocopying, recording, or otherwise, without the prior written permission of the publisher.

Copyright © 1990 by Swets & Zeitlinger B.V., Amsterdam/Lisse

ISBN 90 265 1026 8   ISSN 0924-0578
NUGI 724

CONTENTS

page

Preface — *Michael Vorbeck*

PART 1:

Rapporteur's Report — *Professor John Nisbet*   1

Advice for Authorities Commissioning Evaluation   10

PART 2: COMMISSIONED PAPERS

1 Evaluation from Both Sides of the Same Fence: a case study of the evaluation of the Technical and Vocational Education Initiative
  Harry Black and Gwyneth Deakins (United Kingdom)   11

2 Evaluations: limiting the damage done
  Mogens Jansen (Denmark)   24

3 Evaluation and the Reform of Schools
  Helen Simons (United Kingdom)   46

4 A Structure for Evaluation to Meet the Needs of a Decentralised Reform Strategy in Upper Secondary Education in Sweden
  Lars Johansson (Sweden)   65

5 How Are Evaluations Used Today?
  Andre Hussenet (France)   85

6 The Uses of Evaluation
  Robert Long (United Kingdom)   103

PART 3: SELECTED BACKGROUND REPORTS

Austria
Evaluation of Educational Programmes in Austria
Dr Friedrich Weyermüller — 114

Netherlands
Evaluation of Educational Programmes: state of the art in the Netherlands
Wijnand Th J G Hoeben — 129

Norway
Norwegian Report
Tom Tiller and Ole Briseid — 134

Spain
Spanish Experience with Evaluation in the Educational Field
Mariano Alvaro Page — 138

PART 4: BIBLIOGRAPHY — 144

LIST OF PARTICIPANTS — 158

PREFACE

The North Berwick Workshop was one of a series of educational research meetings which have become an important element in the programme of the Council for Cultural Co-operation of the Council of Europe since 1975. European co-operation in educational research aims at providing Ministries of Education with research findings so as to enable them to prepare their policy decisions. Co-operation should also lead to a joint European evaluation of certain educational reforms, and the theme *Evaluation Of Education Programmes* chosen for the Workshop must be seen in this context.

The educational research meetings bring together research workers and sometimes also administrators from a selected number of the 25 countries taking part in the work of the Council for Cultural Co-operation. The purpose is to compare research findings and experience on a particular topic of current interest.

In the case of the present Workshop the aims were:

To take stock of ongoing or completed evaluation activities in the participating countries and the purposes lying behind their instigation;

To analyse different approaches to and methods of evaluations;

To sound possibilities of European co-operation in this area;

To develop certain guidelines for both those who carry out evaluations and those who use them.

The Workshop was organised by the Scottish Council for Research in Education (SCRE) in co-operation with the Council for Cultural Co-operation. It marked the 60th anniversary of SCRE. The meeting held at the Marine Hotel at North Berwick goes back to a suggestion made in September 1987 by Dr Sally Brown, Director of SCRE, at a Colloquy of Educational Research Directors in Strasbourg. Both SCRE and the Council for Cultural Co-operation agree on the need for regular scrutiny of educational practice and clues to better ways of proceeding, stressed by Mr Gordon Kirk, Chairman of SCRE, at the opening session. Educational systems are suffering pressure for greater efficiency. Evaluation, therefore, has a key role to play, as research for enhanced quality. The ways and means of investigation have to be redefined continuously.

The Workshop discussed the following aspects:
Why we have evaluations;
How we do evaluations;
How evaluations are actually used;
How to get the most out of evaluations.

The following countries were represented: Austria, Belgium, Canada, Denmark, France, Federal Republic of Germany, Greece, Iceland, Luxembourg, Netherlands, Norway, Portugal, Sweden and the United Kingdom. There were also observers from the Nordic Council and the World Confederation of Organisations of the Teaching Profession. The list of participants is given at the end of this book.

Six commissioned papers (covering Denmark, France, Sweden and the United Kingdom) were presented in plenary session and then discussed in three working groups. National and individual reports from various countries, as well as lists of research projects and bibliographies, were tabled as background material. On the final day, the Rapporteur General, Professor John Nisbet from the University of Aberdeen, summed up the situation and the conclusions emerging from the Workshop.

An attempt was also made to offer advice for authorities commissioning evaluation. This is to be found following the Rapporteur's report.

The Council of Europe is particularly grateful to SCRE (Mr Gordon Kirk, Dr Sally Brown, Mrs Pamela Munn, Mr Harry Black, Ms Rosemary Wake, Mr David Gilhooly, Mrs Hedda King, Mrs Moira Simpson and Mrs May Young) for their excellent work in preparing and organising the Workshop. The Council of Europe would also like to express its thanks to the Rapporteur General (Professor John Nisbet), to the lecturers and to the group chairmen and rapporteurs. The editing was done by the Scottish Council for Research in Education.

Michael Vorbeck
Head of the Section for Educational
Research and Documentation.

Rapporteur's Report

John Nisbet

In November 1988 the Scottish Council for Research in Education, in cooperation with the Council of Europe's Council for Cultural Cooperation, organised an international workshop on evaluation. One of the aims of the workshop was "to provide a forum for debate between those who carry out evaluations and those who use them". The value of such a forum quickly became clear as the opening sessions revealed many differing interpretations of the word, 'evaluation'. Some saw it as primarily associated with innovation, evaluation being a summative judgment on whether an innovatory programme had proved successful or a formative source of information to guide innovators in the development of their programme - or, more commonly, both of these functions together. Others, however, related evaluation to testing, either in the form of a national programme of tests to monitor standards of academic performance as a measure of the efficiency of the educational system, or in the form of diagnostic testing to identify the specific difficulties and needs of individual students and pupils. Evaluation was also interpreted as a form of accountability, emphasising the obligation of those employed in the educational system to be answerable to parents, administrators, taxpayers and to the students themselves. In this sense, evaluation is an instrument of management and control. But evaluation can also be interpreted as an integral part of the professional role of teachers, recognising teachers' own responsibility for monitoring their own performance. In this sense, evaluation is an essential element in professional development, enabling teachers to improve the quality of teaching.

Evaluation thus proves to be a global term, an 'evolving concept' as Dr Sally Brown described it in her opening remarks. Educational concepts have a tendency to spread their meaning: 'curriculum', for example, is a term which is now used with such a broad meaning that it has come to mean almost the same as 'education'. The analogy with 'curriculum' also illustrates another point, that those involved in evaluation have to be aware of possible conflict between intended and actual outcomes, balancing consideration of intended purposes with a sensitivity to the actual influence of evaluation on those who are evaluated. The first sessions of the workshop produced so many different interpretations of 'evaluation' that participants quite naturally felt confusion and even frustration. A prime task of the workshop, therefore, was to establish some order out of confusion, by identifying a conceptual framework which would assist mutual understanding and communication.

This report aims to summarise the outcomes of discussions in the workshop by the construction of a cognitive map of the concept of 'evaluation'. The map was not a product of the discussions: it is presented here as a way of representing the experience of those participating in the workshop. Like travellers, we each brought our own mental picture of our experiences in exploring the concept of evaluation, and the map is designed to bring these differing interpretations together in a coherent and helpful structure.

Three questions were posed as a structure for the series of discussions: why do we have evaluations? how do we do evaluations? and how do we use evaluations? If evaluation is interpreted as a global term, the answers to these questions become too general to offer any guide to decisions. Why evaluation? - for a variety of purposes; how? - by a variety of methods; and, to what use should the results be put? - a variety of uses. This is of little help. However, it is possible to pass quickly through this exploratory stage of discussion and review, and move towards identifying underlying principles and concepts, to structure the field so that those who plan, do or use evaluations may have a clearer idea of where they stand in relation to the range of interpretations and applications of evaluation.

It proved not too difficult to agree on certain points of principle at a relatively low level of abstraction. For example, all agreed that the choice of method or style of evaluation depends on its purpose and intended audience. Again, those who are the subject of evaluation should be associated in decisions about the design, conduct and interpretation of the evaluation. The value of feedback to all concerned at the beginning, during and at the end of evaluation was also accepted and emphasised. Negotiation too is a necessary element in evaluation at all stages. Guiding principles such as these are, of course, open to debate, but command a large measure of support. Their main weakness, however, is that they often prove to be incompatible. Thus, the principle of involving participants in an open style of evaluation cannot easily be reconciled with the need to respect confidentiality and to win credibility for the findings. An intention to share results with those who are evaluated has to be set against the claims of those who commission the evaluation to have prior knowledge and even to have ownership of the results.

In the choice between an internal evaluator, who has personal knowledge through involvement, and an external evaluator who is 'uncontaminated', there are sound arguments on both sides. The discussion groups in the workshop quickly agreed that a crucial question is, "What is the purpose of the evaluation?" since purpose determines method and use; but even this leaves questions unanswered - whose purpose? for whose benefit? and who decides and by what criteria? If the objective is effective management, what is 'effective'? - at less cost, or better learning? and who decides what is 'better'? Evaluation necessarily involves judgment; but who makes that judgment is a question in which power, responsibility, fairness, validity and professional expertise all can make their differing claims.

When people meet to discuss evaluation, they quickly discover that their differences of opinion and interpretation reflect deeper divisions in attitudes to authority and accountability, in values concerning human relationships and in beliefs about how best to influence and persuade. From the start, the discussion identified a tension between two uses of evaluation: evaluation for accountability and evaluation for professional development. Evaluation for accountability is the more readily acknowledged aspect, for we tend to perceive evaluation as a form of judgment on competence and efficiency. This is evaluation looking outwards to some external authority. But there is also a personal or inward-directed form of evaluation which is an integral part of professionalism, the acceptance of responsibility for one's own judgment.

> Standards are the most effective when we set them ourselves ... Professionalism requires from us the capacity to apply the highest standards to ourselves even when there is no one but ourselves to judge ... This is what we try to teach our students ... They learn (or do not learn) from our example. (Nisbet, 1986)

The paper by Simons expressed this self-evaluation as follows:

> Professionals are accountable not only to their pupils and colleagues, but to the community they serve as well ... But the professionalism I have in mind to which a growing number of teachers now aspire means much more than this. These professionals evaluate what they do against self-generated critical standards, they research shortfalls in provision and performance ... they experiment, they reflect ... they engage in persuasive

> negotiation with the constituencies whose support and approval they need. It is a responsive community-based professionalism ... (Simons, page 11)

Long, introducing his paper which described a self-evaluation procedure in his area of Oxfordshire (UK), spoke of 'creating a culture of review and reflection which helps teachers to cope with change'. The Oxfordshire programme starts from self-evaluation, and then brings in others ("critical friends") to aid reflection and provide feedback, so as to identify areas of growth and development.

This style of evaluation stands in sharp contrast to national programmes of curriculum reform (see the paper by Hussenet) and of testing (see the paper by Johansson). But these national programmes also recognise that the responsibility for implementation rests with individuals who must incorporate the findings as their own.

> Evaluation at school level has the important task of encouraging those taking part in the development work to reflect on and analyse their own activities. (Johansson, page 13)

The tension between evaluation as an instrument of management or control and evaluation as a means to enhanced professionalism and staff development, between accountability to society and accountability to one's self, provides one possible basis for interpreting the discussions in the workshop. Many other aspects were, of course, raised, and the outcomes of debate on these specific points are set out in the reports of the group discussions. The technique to be used here is to attempt to draw a cognitive map. The purpose of such a map is to extract from the record of discussion a framework within which we can chart the various meanings of evaluation. In this technique, one writes down all the concepts which have been mentioned, and then one tries to group concepts together in clusters, or to identify linkages. From this exercise, finally, a search is made for underlying dimensions which can be used to interpret the meaning we attach to 'evaluation'.

My cognitive map, constructed after several re-arrangements and groupings to reflect the views expressed in discussion, is presented as Figure 1. Here, a selection of terms is set out around the central concept of evaluation: formative, summative, external, internal, appraisal, testing, objectives, planning, top-down models, grass-roots development, product and process, and so on.

Figure 1: EVALUATION — a cognitive map

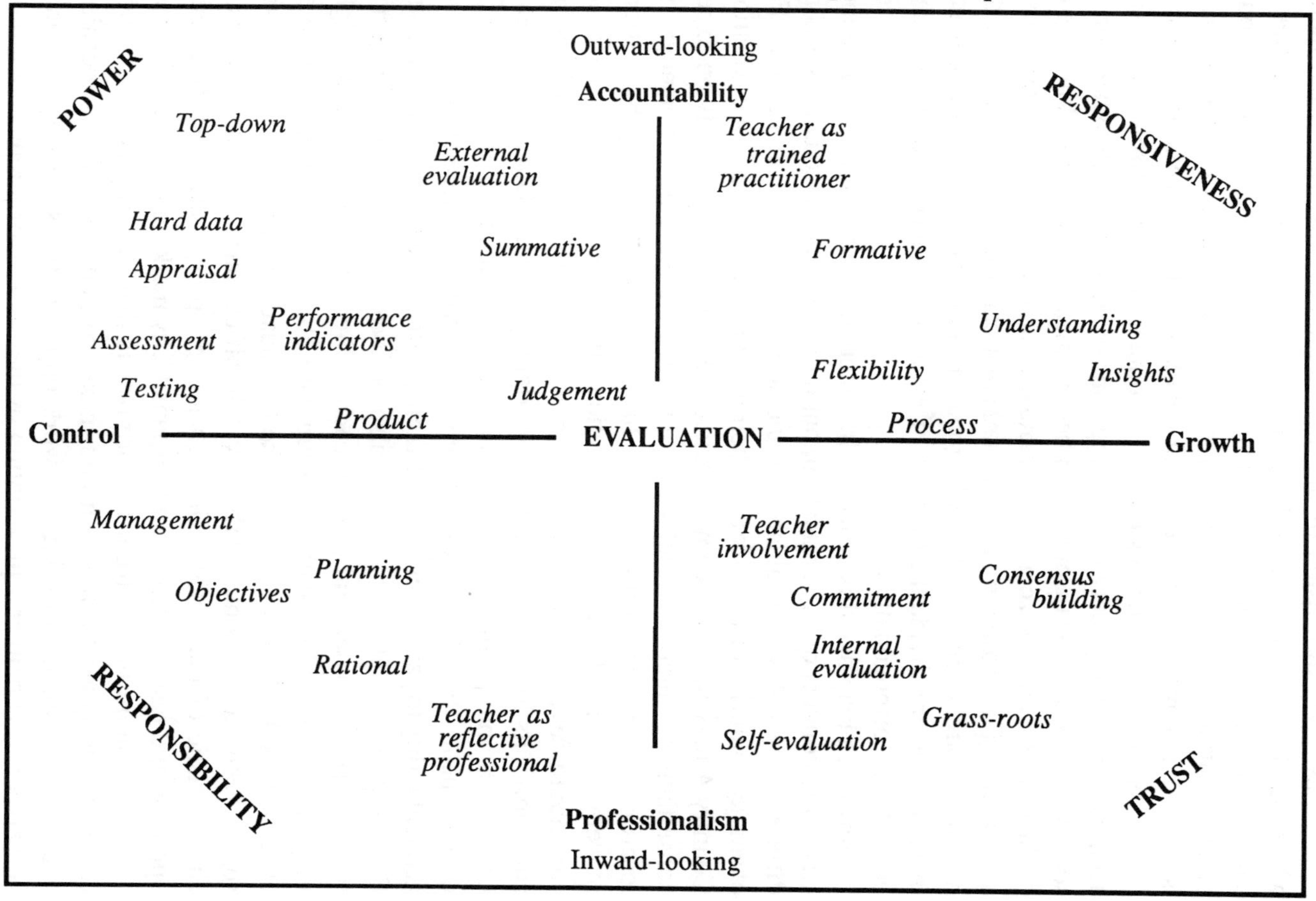

POWER

Top-down
Hard data
Appraisal
Performance indicators
Assessment
Testing

External evaluation
Summative

RESPONSIVENESS

Outward-looking
Accountability

Teacher as trained practitioner
Formative
Understanding
Flexibility
Insights

Control —— Product —— Judgement —— EVALUATION —— Process —— Growth

Management
Objectives
Planning
Rational

Teacher as reflective professional

Teacher involvement
Commitment
Internal evaluation
Consensus building
Self-evaluation
Grass-roots

RESPONSIBILITY

Professionalism
Inward-looking

TRUST

The East-West dimension of the map is control and growth, the theme which has been elaborated in the preceding paragraphs. At one extreme, evaluation may be seen as an instrument of management of educational systems, national or specific, large or small. At the other extreme, evaluation is viewed as a means to professional development, a process of growth.

The North-South dimension is accountability and professionalism, accountability being outward-looking, an accountability to others or to society, and professionalism as used here to mean an inward-looking use of evaluation as a check on one's own standards, an accountability to one's self, as it were. (For those who have a mathematical bent, we concede that the dimensions are not necessarily orthogonal. But the four quadrants into which these dimensions divide the map are of equal importance, and so they have been drawn orthogonally.)

How can a map like this be used? Its function is not to provide guidelines on how to conduct or use evaluation, but rather as a means to understanding different views of what evaluation is and how it should, or can, be used. For example, countries differ widely in their interpretation and use of evaluation. Country A may have a system of national testing and tend to rely on expert consultants to interpret results and advise on improving efficiency: its location is in the top left quadrant. In Country B, there may be a strong movement which favours self-evaluation, using the school as a basis for curriculum development, arguing for a substantial measure of professional autonomy: its location is in the bottom right quadrant. Other personnel in Country B may sympathise with the idea of evaluation as a means to development, but have reservations, favouring a greater degree of accountability to parents and public: their position is in the top right quadrant. Evaluation of specific projects can also be located on the map: Project X which is school-based and largely teacher-directed, is in the bottom right; Project Y, directed by a national group with objective measures to evaluate outcomes, is diagonally opposite. The four quadrants may be labelled (with some hesitation about arbitrary classifications) by the dominant characteristic of the concepts in each group: power and trust diagonally opposite, and responsiveness and responsibility marking the other diagonal.

A key feature of this form of portrayal is that the map is a theoretical construct, designed to draw out and make explicit the different meanings attached to evaluation during the workshop. It shows how evaluation is perceived: it is neither a prescription of the 'ideal' nor a representation of 'actuality'. One of the comments made in discussion (by Johansson) was that, in evaluation, 'interest goes where the money is'. Review of the map suggests that, in 'actuality', the top left quadrant exercises a gravitational pull: action goes where the power is. Thus the map can be used to show to those with power that they are not using their power to sustain all the ideas and values to which they often pay lip-service.

Some participants pointed out that the extremes of the dimensions are not irreconcilable opposites. 'Accountability', for example, is an element in the ideal of 'professionalism'; professionalism must include the idea of public accountability as well as personal professional integrity. Likewise, 'control', it may be argued, is a means to promote 'growth'. The map, however, merely illustrates that these concepts were perceived as opposing extremes. (Perhaps, speculatively, the answer to this criticism of the map would be to represent it as a spherical model, in which the extremes meet by further extrapolation in curved space.)

Is it possible to embrace all the various meanings of evaluation in an ideal understanding, placing 'evaluation' in the middle position of the map? This was the challenge facing the discussion groups in the workshop, to achieve a balance among these various and conflicting requirements. A crucial concept is 'empowerment': who gains power from evaluation, or who is given power to influence change through evaluation? Power is exercised at all stages in evaluation, in deciding the questions to be asked and the kind of evidence to be gathered, in interpreting the data and in implementing the conclusions reached. These decisions may be made in such a way as to empower the professional or the customer (parent or student) or the administrator. Whichever style of evaluation is selected, the claims of each of these groups must be balanced. Formal external evaluation must involve all participants to ensure the implementation of its findings. Self-evaluation is not just a private professional concern, but should also be seen as a management strategy to stimulate institutional change.

The answer then is that evaluation should be a shared responsibility among those who commission evaluation, those who evaluate and those who are evaluated. The discussion groups aimed to formulate advice to evaluators and to the commissioners of evaluation. For the evaluators, the advice is to look inwards and also to look outwards: to be reflective, analytic, prepared to go beyond the precise remit if the remit is too restrictive to provide a comprehensive understanding; but also to be responsive, sensitive to the requirements of different audiences to whom the evaluation is directed. For those who commission evaluation, the advice is to be open-minded and flexible, recognising that it is helpful to be given a new perspective which enables them to see a situation from someone else's viewpoint.

Three other suggestions are relevant to the task of establishing a 'middle position' for evaluation: the evaluator should be independent of the decision-making process; those being evaluated should share "ownership"; and since no one approach and no one perspective has a monopoly of truth, it is wise to adopt more than one style of evaluation.

Total independence from the decision-making process is difficult for the evaluator to achieve, not only because of the pressures of power and funding but also because of the need for evaluation to address itself directly to the issues which decision-makers see as important. While recognising that it is impossible to be wholly neutral, evaluators must distance themselves from all those involved. Yet they must be (and be seen to be) sympathetic to the concerns of all involved, or at least to understand these concerns. This is not as paradoxical as it may seem, for it represents a middle position on the dimension between 'responsive' and 'responsible'. But it leaves difficult issues unresolved; and not all evaluators would agree with a balancing of 'responsive' and 'responsible' in this way.

Most evaluators, however, would agree that those being evaluated should feel some degree of 'ownership' of the evaluation. A sense of ownership is not just a cosmetic applied to make a threatening process more acceptable. It is especially important if those who are evaluated are the persons who will subsequently be expected to implement the findings. If they are to be motivated to implement change, they must feel that their interests have been recognised and their perspectives understood. There is a sense in which only I can change myself. Others can apply pressure to make me accept change. They can force me to change, but then they must maintain the pressure. Persuade me, and the pressure is unnecessary.

Points such as these were made - and disputed - frequently in the course of the workshop. A focus of special attention was the process of 'self-evaluation', the use of evaluation not as an instrument of control but rather as an instrument of professional development, encouraging teachers to be their own critics.

> If (evaluation) can be developed so as to provide teachers - and administrators and parents and all those concerned with education - with the means of improving their own understanding, then its effect will be to put educational studies into a questioning framework ... This is no small task, but one well worth attempting. (Broadfoot & Nisbet, 1981)

However, self-evaluation by itself clearly has serious weaknesses: it lacks credibility, is difficult to manage, involves unfamiliar new skills, depends on openness in relationships, is readily trivialised into marginal issues and may in the end fail to result in genuine improvement. In listing the limitations of external evaluation, we must also acknowledge the potential weaknesses of this form of internal evaluation. Consequently, most evaluations must employ a variety of methods, and where self-evaluation is adopted, it should be paralleled by some form of external evaluation, to strengthen credibility, as a check, and to ensure due recognition of accountability to the concerns of others.

The discussions in the workshop demonstrated how difficult it is to design a procedure for evaluation which occupies the 'middle position' and satisfies the requirements of all the clients and participants in the process. A solution which several discussion groups favoured was to have a written contract, drawn up and agreed before the evaluation is begun. This is clearly important, but as some groups noted, something more is needed. There has to be a continuing process of negotiation throughout the evaluation, a 'permanent dialogue', as one group expressed it - for evaluation is a developing process and understanding evolves slowly. 'Things take time', as Jansen said in his paper to the workshop.

So we need to add to the map the concept of 'communication' - communication among those who commission, those who evaluate and those who are evaluated. Communication implies dialogue and sharing and openness. It is on this basis that we can best develop the process of evaluation, so that it is not just a mechanism of control and management but can become an instrument for growth and development.

Acknowledgments
Comments on the first version of this report are gratefully acknowledged from Sydney Smyth, Helen Simons, James Kidd, Joyce Watt, Martin Merson and Seamus Hegarty.

References
BROADFOOT P. *and* NISBET J. (1981) The impact of research on educational studies. *British Journal of Educational Studies*, 29, 115-122.

NISBET, J. (1986) Staff and standards. In Moodie G C, *Standards and Criteria in Higher Education:* Society for Research into Higher Education and NFER-Nelson, 90-106.

ADVICE FOR AUTHORITIES COMMISSIONING EVALUATION

1. It is important that the purposes of an evaluation be clearly articulated at the outset.

2. It should be recognised that there can be a wide range of purposes for evaluation. The choice of purposes may dictate the nature of the questions which can or should be asked. It will also determine the uses to which the outcome may be put, as well as the style of presentation.

3. There are substantial benefits to be gained by allowing time for meaningful negotiation between the sponsor and the evaluator to clarify the focus of an evaluation.

4. Negotiation on and clarification of those issues should be a feature of all contracts for evaluation. These contracts should be written.

5. Evaluation will be more effective if there is confidence in the relationship between sponsors and evaluators. Confidence can be nurtured by avoiding the misuse of evaluation data (eg selective interpretation or reporting of findings).

6. Users, participants, evaluators and commissioners all have rights and obligations which have to be negotiated from the outset. There should be a permanent dialogue between those who commission, those who evaluate and those who are evaluated.

1
Evaluation from Both Sides of the Same Fence
A Case Study of the Evaluation of the Technical and Vocational Education Initiative

Harry Black, SCRE, Edinburgh

Gwyneth Deakins, TVEI Unit, Department of Employment, London

ABSTRACT: The paper sets out to explore why evaluations are commissioned and to examine a real example of the independent external evaluation of an innovatory programme. It identifies potential beneficiaries as being not only policy-makers but other interested parties such as students, parents, employers and teachers. Evaluation can offer information and insight which can be used for preparative, formative and summative purposes. It can record the success and failure of the strategies adopted and it establishes an ethos of commitment. However, in some cases it does not fulfil its potential and becomes little more than a bureaucratic exercise.

The Technical and Vocational Education Initiative which is the focus of the case study was evaluated to provide formative information to policy-makers both in the sponsoring agency and elsewhere. It comprised a number of databases and a programme of qualitative studies on a range of topics. In addition to the national programme, the sponsors provided funds for the local evaluation of individual projects, to be used at the discretion of the local authority.

The TVEI evaluation programme has provided information which offers not only a description of how the Initiative has progressed but also a source of objective information on aspects of good practice and alternative strategies. It has been effective in disseminating findings about TVEI both through formal reports and conferences as well as through the evaluators themselves as they go about their work. It has also emphasised the Training Agency's commitment to quality both in the educational world and amongst other government departments.

At the same time, the paper recognises that the evaluation programme could have been managed to greater effect and acknowledges that it is easier to describe what was carried out than to identify what policy decisions have been taken or changed as a direct result of its findings. It concludes with three lessons which could be derived from the experience. These include the need for a mechanism to consider and act on findings, the need for the evaluation to focus with greater flexibility on the critical objectives of the programme, and the need for an effective strategy to disseminate findings in such a way that those who provide the information consider their efforts to be worthwhile.

The views expressed in this paper are those of the writers and do not necessarily represent the views of the Scottish Council for Research in Education nor the Department of Employment.

WHY DO WE HAVE EVALUATION?

To begin with we have to establish that there are many reasons why evaluations are conducted in education. Evaluations can focus on existing programmes or systems, on educational innovations, or on specific materials such as school textbooks or audio-visual aids. They can be carried out by external agents, by individuals with an evaluation remit within institutions, or indeed by the whole institution for the purpose of 'self-evaluation'. They can be conducted to inform policy-makers, practitioners, users or other interested parties. We could go on making distinctions amongst, for example, formative and summative purposes or about the different roles which can be taken by the evaluator, but the fundamental message is clear - 'evaluation' as it is used in British education today is a complex term.

During this conference we will have ample opportunities to explore these various nuances, but the purpose of this paper is to offer a real case study of evaluation and to explore how it relates to the 'theory'. It is the case study of the independent external evaluation of an innovatory programme: the

Technical and Vocational Education Initiative (TVEI). The extent to which it has implications for other aspects of evaluation will become clear as the conference progresses.

TVEI is a major initiative in schools and colleges, funded through the Training Agency - that is, a part of the Department of Employment and not of the Department of Education. Its general aim is to give young people between the ages of 14 and 18 a wider and richer education to prepare them better for adult and working life, and originates in the Government's concern to produce a more skilled and adaptable workforce. Specifically it aims, for example, to 'encourage more young people to seek and obtain qualifications or skills which will be of direct value to them at work', to develop their initiative, motivation and enterprise and problem-solving skills, and also to develop closer links between the world of education and industry so that the curriculum has the confidence of industry.

The Initiative was started as a five-year pilot scheme, with TVEI projects in 14 education authorities in 1983. The exact nature and content of each project varied according to the needs and circumstances of each authority, but in general all projects were supposed to offer four-year programmes to a cohort of students from across the ability range, emphasising equal opportunities for boys and girls and including an element of work experience in outside industry and commerce. In addition, significant numbers of new and enhanced curriculum options have been developed under TVEI, mainly in the fields of craft, technology, computing and pre-vocational studies.

The number of TVEI pilot projects was increased with 48 joining in 1984, 12 in 1985 and 21 in 1986. In 1987 the Initiative was 'extended' from the pilot projects to include whole authorities; the first 11 education authorities to enter 'extension' did so in 1987 and under the present programme all education authorities in Britain, and hence all pupils 14-18, will be covered by TVEI by 1997.

The pilot phase of TVEI was covered by a comprehensive programme of evaluation, and it is from this that we draw the experiences and conclusions which we relate here today.

Questions for the paper
The theme we were asked to consider was 'Why do we have evaluation?' To do this in our case study we will address five questions. These comprise:
1 Who **might** benefit from an evaluation of TVEI?
2 **What** might an evaluation offer them?
3 Why was an evaluation of **TVEI** commissioned?

4   What was the nature of the TVEI evaluation **programme**?
5   What, on reflection, have proved to be the **benefits** of choosing to evaluate TVEI?

Who might benefit from evaluation?
There has been a tradition in educational evaluation to accept the adage that 'he who pays the piper calls the tune'. As it is normally the agency sponsoring the innovation which provides the funds, it is not surprising that most writing about evaluation identifies it closely with the needs of the 'decision-maker' (Cronbach 1982). While there is little empirical evidence on the use of evaluations in the United Kingdom, it can reasonably be assumed that in most cases it is 'decision-makers' who are seen as at least the first audience for most evaluation reports in this country.

But it would be wrong to assume that 'providing information to decision-makers' constitutes an uncontroversial *status quo*, particularly if the concept of 'decision-maker' is a restrictive one. For example, in the United States where professional 'Standards for Evaluation of Educational Programs, Projects and Materials' have been enunciated (Joint Committee on Standards for Educational Evaluation, 1981) the practice of 'responding to the concerns of one interest group more than another' has been recognised as unacceptable. Yet a study by Newman and Brown (1987) identified this as the second most frequently-cited violation of standards amongst 147 respondents. Similarly, in the United Kingdom since the 1970s there has been a growing recognition that evaluation can and should relate to the needs of diverse audiences (MacDonald 1974) such as students, parents, employers and teachers.

We can therefore take as a reasonable starting point an assumption that many interested parties might benefit from evaluation. The complication, of course, is that these diverse audiences may wish to answer the question 'Why do we have evaluations?' in different ways. Parlett and Hamilton (1972), for example, noted that

> The participants will be anxious to correct deficiencies, make improvements and establish future priorities. The sponsors and board members will be concerned with pedagogic issues but will also want to know about the innovation's costs, use of resources and outside reputation. The outsiders will read the report to decide whether or not the scheme has 'worked', or to see whether it could be applied or adapted to their own situation.

Parlett and Hamilton go on to argue that because of the varied criteria for success which these groups may have, it is not easy to provide a simple 'yes' or 'no' on the innovation's future. This clearly raises the question about what an evaluation can provide.

What might an evaluation offer?
The unique contributions which professional external evaluation offers are independent **information** and **insight** which can be used for a number of **purposes**. We will consider each of these in turn.

Perhaps the most obvious rationale for choosing to have evaluations is to provide **information**. This information can 'measure' success in achieving goals, in meeting performance criteria and in providing 'value for money'. It can provide a description of what is happening on the ground and of the effects of policy decisions. It can offer a resource which will help policy-makers make decisions and allow others to monitor progress for their own purposes.

Raw data are, however, no more than the building bricks of the **process** of evaluation. These data can be analysed to provide **insight**. By choosing to devote resources to evaluation, the sponsors of an innovation are ensuring that time will be made available for selected individuals or groups to be reflective about what is taking place. Independent external evaluators have thus become what Kushner and MacDonald (1987) have called 'the storytellers and theorists of innovation'. Their role, according to Cronbach (1982) is to 'speed up the learning process by communicating what might otherwise be overlooked or wrongly perceived' and, accordingly, 'An evaluation ought to reduce uncertainties, but it should also challenge simplistic views'.

Of course, it could be argued that the opportunity to offer such insights is not unique to the evaluator. Other participants in the process of evaluation can offer insights, and although these may be less unbiased than those obtainable from external evaluators, they may be grounded in a depth of knowledge unavailable to the evaluator, especially when resources are limited. However, the independence of the evaluator offers **access** to data which may not otherwise be available. This access is not only to groups such as parents or employers, who are inaccessible in any systematic way to most project managers; it is also access to the insights of participants who may be close to the centre but whose independent views are little known because of the group dynamics of most decision-making processes.

Evaluation data, which in its widest sense encompasses both information and insight, can thus be used to inform decisions. In evaluation as we know it in the UK today, these decisions will fall into two groups. On the one hand they may be 'formative' and thus appropriate to the on-going development of the innovation. On the other they may be 'summative' and thus relate to the judgements which must be made when longer-term decisions about 'success', 'failure', 'impact' or 'outcome' must be made.

The important caveat to this neat dichotomy is that although evaluations **can** be used in this way, there is a lack of evidence to confirm that they always are. Indeed, Alkin (1975) has identified four contexts in which there is no intention that evaluation should relate to the decision-making process, including those where

(a) the evaluation is no more than 'window-dressing' to justify decisions which have already been made

(b) there is a contractual obligation to carry out an evaluation although it is seen by the innovators as no more than a bureaucratic inconvenience

(c) it is the public relations effect of commissioning an evaluation which counts although there is no intention of using the outcomes, and

(d) the commissioner identifies potential *kudos* in having a reputation as an innovator but will only use the evaluation outcomes if they are clearly supportive of his or her strategies.

Recognition of the uneasy tension between the **intention** that evaluation should inform the decision-making process, and the reality that it does not always seem to do so, is no new contribution to knowledge (Chelimsky, 1987). But it is interesting that the established dichotomy between formative and summative purposes relates only to the ongoing and the final decisions which must be made about innovations. There is little in the literature to suggest that evaluation may be an activity which could **identify** innovations which might be appropriate.

This may be, of course, because evaluators are seldom asked to apply their skills to existing systems. Changes to these systems emerge from a process which Chelimsky considers to be an area as yet little exploited by the evaluation community, at least in the United States where she works. However, as an educational evaluator in the US Congress, she cites a case study of how her work was used to inform a policy decision before it was instigated. It is perhaps unlikely that most professional evaluators will have access to policy-making at such a level. Nevertheless, for those evaluators who despair about the value of their efforts, perhaps we should recognise that in addition to formative and summative purposes there may be a **preparative** purpose which has yet to be fully exploited and which might relate more clearly to the decision-making process.

It would be mistaken, however, to assume that the potential contribution of evaluation is only in the short term. The investment of resources in an innovation is also a learning experience for the innovators. Yet the prime concern of the innovator is to bring the programme to a successful conclusion. There is little motivation for those in that role to record the problems that were encountered, the successful and less successful strategies adopted and the reasons for these. In the long term, without the evaluators' record it will only be those who participate who gain from the experience. The opportunity for an evaluation to disseminate the experience and to leave a record for the future may in itself be sufficient reason to justify its being commissioned.

Finally, it has to be recognised that choosing to commission the external evaluation of an innovation has implications beyond the provision of information and insight. Investment of resources in this way, especially if they come from the funding agency, is a clear statement from the sponsors of a commitment to quality. It establishes an ethos of evaluation for the project which underlines the need for high standards of management and delivery. This may be the 'hidden curriculum' answer to the question 'Why do we have evaluation?' - but it would be difficult to argue that it is not at least as important as the 'formal curriculum' of observation and reports.

Why did the Training Agency choose to evaluate TVEI?
Having set out the general background we must now consider the particular case of TVEI. Why did the Training Agency choose to evaluate it? The short answer, and the one given publicly, is - to see if it worked! Within that, however, there were specific purposes which had a great deal to do with the form of the Initiative when it was set up.

As we noted above, TVEI started as a number of limited pilot projects; it covered a specific cohort of students in selected schools and colleges. Even when the Initiative established projects in a growing number of authorities, the pilot approach was maintained. It was felt to be particularly important at that early stage of an innovative programme that there was a mechanism for assessing how the various aims of TVEI were being met in practice, and using this information both to assist the development of the pilot projects and to disseminate the lessons learnt more widely throughout the education system, so that the principles of TVEI might have wider applications. This is why a system of evaluation of the Initiative at national level was set up, and at the same time each local education authority was given funding to evaluate its own project and examine the lessons learnt.

It is relatively unusual for those who commission evaluation to do so not only for their own direct purposes but also directly to encourage and enable others to evaluate the same programme separately for their own purposes. It is within this context of a formative purpose for the evaluation that a great deal of attention has been given to disseminating the results of both national and local evaluation: for example, through widely published reports and workshops.

Since the beginning of TVEI in 1983, decisions have been taken which have extended TVEI across all education authorities in the country and, ultimately, will extend it to all children in the 14-18 age groups. However, an evaluation which can serve as a means of examining, objectively and in depth, the multitude of innovative practices introduced by TVEI, and of spreading the word about them to other practitioners, continues to have an important role.

The other major purpose of the evaluation was to assist the Training Agency in finding out whether the money it was spending on the Initiative was having the expected effect in terms of meeting the objectives set for it. This is perhaps the more traditional role of evaluation as central government departments tend to see it. The evaluation programme is particularly vital in a programme of this sort which is delivered through agencies - the education authorities - and not directly by officers of the TA itself. The Agency has therefore had few staff of its own 'on the ground', or any standard management information system to provide data on the effectiveness of the programme.

The evaluation and monitoring of TVEI has proved to be one of the major sources of information to senior staff in the Unit, and thence to the Training Agency and other government departments, about what TVEI is achieving.

The TVEI approach to evaluation was relatively new in education in the country; although the education world was used to inspectors, the evaluation was carried out by 'outsiders' and as such was regarded initially with suspicion. It was certainly new to insist that educational authorities and institutions should be developing evaluation of, and for, themselves. It was also a relatively rare practice among government departments generally, although the Training Agency has a tradition of introducing innovative schemes in the employment sphere and of commissioning research to evaluate their effectiveness. However, the evaluation of the TVEI pilots has been more comprehensive than most, and almost unique in its emphasis on feedback and constructive use of its findings by the practitioners. What is interesting is that over the last two or three years much greater emphasis is being placed by central government on evaluation of government policy initiatives - detailed guidance has recently been issued by the Treasury - as pressure increases to have objective examination of programmes to see if they are achieving what they were intended to.

What was the nature of the TVEI monitoring and evaluation programme?
The evaluation programme itself consists, firstly, of national-level evaluation and monitoring, and secondly, of local evaluation. The national evaluation and monitoring is conducted separately in England and Wales from Scotland, where the education system differs and where TVEI was established somewhat later than in the rest of the country (a substantial part of the national evaluation of TVEI in Scotland is carried out by SCRE, our hosts this week). The evaluation and monitoring is carried out by various educational research institutions - often University Departments of Education - under contract to the Training Agency. The overall programme is managed, and its outputs disseminated, by the evaluation section of the TVEI Unit.

The national programme on both sides of the border includes monitoring through the collection of statistical data: there are databases both for details of the curricula followed by TVEI students, and for details of the TVEI students themselves - numbers, gender, ability levels, exam results, for example. Reports are produced periodically which analyse the trends shown by the data.

The qualitative evaluation at national level was intended to cover the Initiative quite comprehensively; a total of 19 questions was posed at the beginning of the Initiative, which it was intended the evaluation would answer. In England and Wales, the programme consisted of two major studies over a period of about three years, one focusing on curriculum change and the other on management and organisation issues. In Scotland, the national evaluation has focused on education/industry links, and on management of change and students' choices and attainments. These studies have all generated a number of published reports on the various aspects of TVEI that have been examined as part of the overall contracts.

As well as the main national programmes, a number of special studies have been commissioned to examine particular issues in more depth: for example, the experience of ethnic minority students in TVEI, work experience and equal opportunities in TVEI. These generate separate reports, which are also usually published.

In addition, under the TVEI pilot programme each local education authority which participated was obliged to undertake a programme of independent evaluation of its own TVEI projects. All authorities were obliged by the contract they signed with the Training Agency to spend at least 1% of the money they received on evaluation. Therefore, throughout the pilot stage of the Initiative each participating authority has had - or should have had - a regular flow of evaluative feedback from independent sources on various aspects of TVEI in their areas. For many authorities it was a new experience to be compelled to look at themselves in this way, and the success of local evaluators and the quality of their work has varied. Nevertheless, the local evaluators' work, in addition to assisting the authorities who have commissioned it, has generated an immense amount of important material on what is happening in TVEI. The material, through local evaluation reports, has been available to the TVEI Unit centrally as well as to LEAs. It is of great relevance to authorities who are considering entering the extension phase of TVEI at the present time.

What have been the benefits of TVEI evaluation?
We finally move to consider what have been the benefits of evaluation from the point of view of TVEI.

There undoubtedly have been benefits. At the most basic level, the evaluation and monitoring programme has provided a considerable and growing body of information about what is going on at all levels in the Initiative, on databases, in written reports and in the expertise built up by the evaluators themselves. It is important to remember that our only other major sources of data are consultant advisers, whose views may be partial and not based on any systematic information-gathering programme.

The information has been used, not simply for descriptive reporting of what TVEI is achieving - important though that is when it comes to justifying the programme in the outside world - but also as a source of information for advisers and practitioners seeking, for example, areas of good practice or alternative strategies for meeting TVEI's objectives. Its value has been in being relatively objective and in having been gathered and reported in a systematic manner.

This has been of critical importance to a programme that has been continually expanding and developing. We have already referred to the emphasis given by the TVEI Unit to the active dissemination of the evaluation findings in conferences and workshops, giving practitioners the chance to discuss the findings with the evaluators and each other. The feedback we receive is that such events are found to be useful in stimulating ideas and sharing experiences. In addition, it has been found that the evaluators have tended to develop an informal dissemination role as they visit school and education authority personnel in the course of their work - an unexpected benefit.

In a more general sense, there could be said to have been a benefit for TVEI in terms of the attitudes and expectations engendered by the fact that the evaluation programme existed at all - perhaps the 'commitment to quality' mentioned earlier. As we have indicated, TVEI evaluation was something of an innovation in the educational field. It would be encouraging to think that it did give a message about the TVEI Unit's genuine concern about, and intention to examine, the quality of the TVEI pilot projects; certainly the Unit's overall policy of holding annual reviews of projects' progress, and insisting on their developing their own evaluation and monitoring, was a startling new concept to many education authorities. It is likely that at least **they** will have benefited from having to develop their thinking and practices in this area, not least because it may have helped them to address the issues raised by other educational initiatives which have followed TVEI.

It could also be said that the existence of an evaluation programme demonstrated to those to whom the Training Agency is directly financially accountable - the Employment Department and the Treasury - that it was seriously and critically assessing whether it was meeting the objectives it had set for the whole programme.

In setting out these benefits, however, one is aware that some aspects of the TVEI evaluation could be said to have come close to the circumstances we outlined earlier, in which there is no intention of actually using the findings of evaluation for a constructive purpose: the public relations exercise, the inconvenience of adverse findings, etc.

For example, it is easier to say that a comprehensive programme of monitoring and evaluation is in place than to identify policy decisions that have been taken or changed solely as a direct result of its findings. To take another example, we have recently found that the dissemination of critical reports is happily accepted until they are reported in the national press. Also, we have known for some time that aspects of the evaluation are regarded as a bureaucratic inconvenience by teachers and project staff.

In order to maximise the benefits from evaluation, we may derive some lessons from the TVEI experience. These may be summarised as follows:

A mechanism for considering and acting upon the conclusions must be built into any evaluation programme from the start - otherwise, the evaluation will be marginalised. This mechanism could have been more effective both at national and at local level.

The evaluation must relate to the critical objectives of the programme being evaluated; the evaluation must therefore be flexible enough to adapt to changing circumstances. Some educational authorities have found it difficult to relate the emerging findings on evaluation of the pilot projects of TVEI to the national extension recently undertaken.

The evaluation findings must be fed back to those who are being evaluated, in a constructive way. The credibility of the whole activity depends on its practitioners' seeing tangible benefits to themselves, or at least a clear and defensible use of the information by others. In the TVEI pilot, some data-gathering activities have generated resentment by causing a great deal of work for little obvious feedback.

The latter two points are the joint responsibility of the evaluators and those who directly manage their work. The first brings us back to many of the points made earlier in our presentation. It is the responsibility of policy-makers to decide how much notice they are going to take of evaluation's findings, and how they will react to adverse criticism.

References

ALKIN, M. C. (1975) Evaluation: who needs it? Who cares? *Studies in Educational Evaluation, 1, 3.*

CHELIMSKY, E. (1987) What have we learned about the politics of program evaluation? *Educational Evaluation and Policy Analysis, 9, 3.*

CRONBACH, L. J. (1982) Issues in planning evaluations. In: CRONBACH, L. J. *Designing Evaluations of Educational and Social Programs.* San Francisco: Jossey-Bass.

JOINT COMMITTEE ON STANDARDS FOR EDUCATIONAL EVALUATION (1981) *Standards for Evaluations of Educational Programs, Projects and Materials.* New York: McGraw-Hill.

KUSHNER, S. *and* MacDONALD, B. (1987) The limitations of programme evaluation. In: MURPHY, R. *and* TORRANCE, H. (eds) *Evaluating Education: issues and methods.* London: Harper and Row.

MacDONALD, B. (1974) Evaluation and the control of education. In: MacDONALD, B. *and* WALKER, R. (eds) *Innovation, Evaluation, Research and the Problem of Control.* Norwich: Centre for Applied Research in Education.

NEWMAN, D. L. *and* BROWN, R. D. (1987) Violations of evaluation standards: frequency and seriousness of occurrence. Paper presented at the annual meeting of AERA, Washington.

PARLETT, M. *and* HAMILTON, D. (1972) *Evaluation as Illumination: a new approach to the study of innovatory programmes,* Occasional paper 9. Edinburgh: Centre for Research in the Educational Sciences.

2
Evaluations: Limiting the Damage Done

Mogens Jansen,
The Danish Institute for Educational Research

WHY DO WE HAVE EVALUATION?
The natural response to the question 'why do we evaluate?' would be 'obviously in order to obtain knowledge!'

An evaluation is primarily of interest to the person who is being evaluated. However, evaluation has a number of other functions:

> it provides *parents* with useful information which will enable them to help their child make important choices;

> it helps the *teacher* organise the instruction;

> it guides the *administrator* in connection with the distribution of resources;

> it supports the *psychologist* in attempting to identify those pupils in need of special education;

> it obtains information for the *researcher*.

The response to the question 'Why do we have evaluation?' should really be as follows: 'It depends on who is carrying out the evaluation'. However, all of those involved in evaluation believe that they obtain knowledge through information. This belief rests, among other things, on the belief in an 'average' as a yardstick.

Parents often feel that they have a claim to know how things are going in school, and the less information they already have about the school and the teaching methods used, the greater their desire to be informed. They also think that they will obtain valuable knowledge through the results of a test. However, parents are even less aware than teachers of just what precisely is measured by a test.

Being able to use tests occasionally makes the teacher feel secure - especially if such tests demonstrate that pupils' achievements in reading (as measured by the test in question) are 'above average', whether a school average, a local average, or a national average.

The *school principal* will ask if the children are learning enough - and there is often the implication that pupils ought to score higher here at the East School than at the West School, because the leadership of the East School is excellent.

Education committees and local politicians are interested to see results showing that the funds invested in the school have proved to be money well spent. They will be delighted to be able to claim that 'Children in this municipality score above the national average!'. Less favourable results are naturally greeted less enthusiastically. Unfortunately, it is not possible for all results at all places to be above the national average.

Central government politicians and administrators think that when, for example, we 'improve the leaving examination after grade ...', 'have spent more money on education than ...', 'have moved resources from ... to ...', the results of the pupils must bear out the wisdom of these policy decisions. People forget that the demands of society are increasing and that the status quo is an expression of a relative increase.

The more institutional power wielded by those observing schools, the more likely they are to think in terms of 'good—>better—>best'. The closer one is to the individual pupil (and especially, if one *is* the pupil), the more interested one is to get answers to questions like 'How is this pupil getting on?' (How am I getting on?) and 'How does this pupil make progress in the subject areas?' (How do I make progress?).

WHO IS EVALUATED? - AND WHO IS NOT?

In any educational system it is traditionally the pupils who are evaluated. The purpose of the evaluation is probably partly to ensure that the pupils get the best possible education, and partly to encourage the pupils. In other words, it's the old story of the carrot and the stick.

There is always the suspicion that evaluation of this type also includes a (hidden) wish to reward or to threaten *teachers*.

Occasionally demands are also made on *parents*. Of course, pupils cannot trade in their parents for new ones, but one might conclude from the knowledge we have today (about the importance of genetic matters, conditions during pregnancy, childbirth, early childhood, the home) that it would be desirable in some instances if pupils were able to get themselves new parents retroactively.

It is crucial that evaluations are directed towards the *education system* as a whole and not just towards teachers. The *education acts* themselves, as well as the people who are financially responsible for their realisation, also ought to be evaluated. In Denmark it is a long and strong historic tradition that the given financial framework is demonstratively badly suited to the educational aims.

The way in which *local school politicians and administrators* implement decisions made by central authorities varies considerably according to local circumstances. Objectively, it would be desirable to evaluate the work of local school politicians and administrators. This is not done in the part of the world that I know best.

Neither is the educational quality of the *teaching materials* evaluated. For instance, in Iceland and Denmark there is not even a tradition of examining the underlying educational and human philosophies of teaching materials even although it is clear that they represent widely differing ideological standpoints. (Jansen & Ahm, 1971; Jansen, 1966; 1969; 1975).

Theories on education are seldom evaluated - and the evaluation of the educational consequences of the theories is even rarer.

Furthermore, *instructional practices* are not often evaluated, although there are exceptions, eg Chall, 1967. At the time it appeared that Chall was evaluating reading methods in general. In retrospect, however, the focus of the book appears to be much narrower and is thus of limited use as a general study in this field. Chall was in fact evaluating reading methods as they were administered during a certain period within a single language area and mainly in one country.

'You can lead a horse to water, but you cannot make it drink' is a salutary reminder that *pupils' motivation* is an important factor to bear in mind when dealing with the evaluation of methods. In reading, my area of special interest, the teacher is not always aware of the fact that the *pupils* are the ones who are supposed to do the work. In many cases the teacher is a much more active person than the pupil.

It is of key importance to evaluate the *subject area activities* that the pupils are *actually* involved in, as there are great differences to be seen here. The area of reading provides a good illustration of this. Although we can distinguish look-and-say methods, phonetic methods, spelling methods, LEA-methods, etc; in the day-to-day routine the methods are often so alike that it is difficult for the classroom teacher to tell the difference. However, the differences among the subject area activities in which the pupils are actually involved may be quite pronounced - irrespective of the method.

The methods used should be devised with the final aim in mind. If this is in fact achieved, the learning outcome is likely to be achieved. By way of example, a method attaching importance to activities which make it possible for the pupils to read a large amount of material chosen by themselves, is valuable when the aim is to make the pupils good readers (Kreiner, 1986).

WHAT PARTS OF SUBJECTS ARE EVALUATED?
In Denmark the teaching of Danish has a high priority in the educational system. The school curriculum has a broad base, and includes mathematics, foreign languages, science, natural science, social science, arts, etc. However, Danish (like English in the UK) has pride of place. Therefore, this subject is chosen as an example - also because it is the one that I know best, to be honest.

When describing the teaching of Danish in Denmark it is traditional to divide it into five areas:
1 verbal expression;
2 reading;
3 written expression;
4 spelling;
5 handwriting.

The division is artificial and inapplicable in practice. Nevertheless we use it. It may be useful when we want to look into *what* is evaluated within the Danish instruction:
1 There is general agreement that it is hopeless to aim at evaluating *verbal expression* with a fair degree of precision. It is done, however, and views about how effectively children communicate orally differ considerably.

   On the one hand, there is the view that 'The language of the children is getting even worse - more simple! Soon the children will only be able to speak in comic balloons. It was not like that when I went to school.'

   On the other hand, there is the belief that children express themselves better than adults: 'The children of today speak more clearly, are more able to take an active part in discussions, than I at that age.'

   These views might both be right - or perhaps neither of them is right. However, the evaluation we have been able to produce so far within the field has been little more than 'clarifying conceptually at an extremely introductory level' - to put it positively.

2. We evaluate *reading,* and to some degree it *is* possible to evaluate pupils' competence in reading. At least we do so. But do we evaluate reading aloud and/or silent reading? Do we evaluate reading for comprehension of the broad meaning of the material, or do we concentrate on pupils grasping minute details?
3. It is difficult, perhaps inadvisable, to aim at evaluating *written expression.* At best the results are 'variable' - to put it diplomatically.
4. It is possible to evaluate competence in Danish *spelling* very precisely. A dictionary of 622 pages is the final judge of what is right and wrong, and there is no possibility of appeal (Dansk Sprognaevn, 1986). Every year in the month of May there is discussion about what is right or wrong. The fact is that far more variants are allowed in spelling than parents, writers, journalists and school politicians will ever know. From time to time the people who prepare the annual spelling test after grade 9 are suspected of seeking out words for the test which expose lack of knowledge at a very high level, sometimes as high up as the level of ministers and Folketing. As I myself am in charge of this field, I can say that we do not compile the annual spelling test in order to trick anyone. However, we know very well that some discussion will always follow.
5. *Handwriting* cannot be evaluated, although some people still use aesthetic criteria to judge it. Others are of the opinion that the main criterion for evaluation should be whether the piece of writing communicates effectively. I agree with the latter, but so far I have seen no measuring device.

Of the five areas of Danish language teaching, which might be evaluated, area 4 can be evaluated with certainty, and area 2 with some degree of certainty. Areas 1 and 5 cannot be evaluated, and area 3 is being evaluated, even if it is inadvisable to so do. In other words, only parts, *sections,* of a subject area are evaluated.

HOW DO WE EVALUATE?
Through observation
This question is occasionally and erroneously reduced to 'What tests do we use for the evaluation, and how do we process the results?' Then these tests are discussed in detail. However, there are many other possible ways of evaluating. For example, observation of the instruction of the pupils would be useful if carried out routinely by the teacher and as a matter of course in the

everyday life in school.

As it is, all good teachers routinely observe their pupils anyway. This can be illustrated by examples from reading. Naturally the teacher notices how effectively pupils read textbooks. Furthermore, the teacher knows something about the reading habits of pupils - how many books they borrow from the school library and the public library, and how much they read. The teacher is aware of pupils' reading habits at home. There is discussion in class about what the pupils are about to read, what they are reading, and what they have read.

Such observations are *valuable* - educationally. Sometimes they are not just seen as being personal impressions on the part of the teacher, but rather as indisputable 'facts'. However, that Ann is a poor reader is perhaps 'in reality' due to the fact that she is asked to read texts which she rejects as too difficult or uninteresting according to her experience and general background. Perhaps if she were given more appropriate reading material she would be encouraged to become a more competent reader.

Apart from Ann's reading, perhaps also her *reading matter* (books provided by the school) ought to be evaluated as well as the way reading is taught. Or perhaps the problem is that Ann's home is totally devoid of texts other than those that emerge on the groceries in the kitchen or on the television? If Ann's reading is to improve on a permanent basis, perhaps it is the *background* of her reading competence that ought to be evaluated - with a view to effecting changes?

I will now go on to look at how this might be achieved.

Through reading tests
First of all it is necessary to know 'which kind of reading' is being evaluated. By way of example, *reading aloud tests* aim at evaluating a kind of reading where the pupil's pronunciation, etc. forms part of a complex picture. And on the basis of something that is heard, something about reading comprehension is deduced. *Silent reading tests* evaluate how well the pupil masters the written language; however, the efficacy of this reading is determined in different ways, eg by multiple choice, closed and open questions. It is essential to know how well such tasks have been 'drilled' through the materials used in day-to-day teaching, since these tests operate on the basis of how the pupil is taught.

Nevertheless, in some instances, where at least some of these factors have been taken into consideration, test data have been used with valuable effect. This is because teachers, reading consultants and psychologists, regardless of the psychometric test guidelines, have related results of their daily observations with other impressions of the pupils' way of reading, with the test and with their general knowledge of the pupils. A variety of sources has been drawn on to build up an accurate picture of how a pupil is actually getting on.

The comparison of many kinds of data in this way, and the spontaneous or systematic weighing of their inter-relationships has (in Denmark) often been part of individual testing in special education and has not been of much interest to teachers in the ordinary education system. However, new strategies are being developed in the classroom and educational development and change is no longer merely in the minds of the curriculum planners. Teachers' knowledge and awareness of educational matters is increasing; for these reasons many are now interested in using observations systematically in their ordinary class teaching.

Through a variety of methods

A continuum of evaluation could be outlined as follows: it goes from the teacher's informal observation of pupils' use of books and their reading habits, via the teacher listening to pupils reading aloud and using informal reading tests to the point where the teacher builds up a picture of what the child reads apart from textbooks.

The sequence of evaluation continues via the use of reading testing texts and to the use of group tests in silent reading - and ends with very objective individual tests worked out with a specific diagnostic purpose.

The question 'how do we evaluate?' is thus an extremely complex one. It should also be mentioned that the contents of the tests vary, both as regards subjects and concepts. Great importance is attached to:

> what the pupil is able to read and comprehend;
> what the pupil is just about to become able to read with understanding;
> what the pupil does not master.

The answers to each of these three issues have implications for the methods and materials used. And there are other points to be made. For example, it should also be clear that the reading process cannot only be seen on the basis of the difficulty of a text, but also in relation to the reader's purpose. Above all, we must look at what motivates the reader to read in the first place.

The concept of 'reading' includes *being able* to read, *daring* to read, *wanting* to read - and actually *doing* it.

So far we have only been concerned with reading tests used in the mainstream educational system. In the case of special education, other and far more individually oriented tests come into focus; but that is a different story altogether, and one which we do not have time to look into in the present context.

TESTS - POSITIVELY ASSESSED
Tests may have a positive effect on teaching
Tests are tools of observation. They may provide short cuts to valuable observation. Ideally, they are time-saving, and they may be useful in situations where their possibilities and limits are clearly defined.

Standardised tests can often be used with good effect. They must be adjusted constantly in order not to become obsolete and misleading. This is necessary because conditions in society change. When this happens, the pupil's own environment changes. This means that educational goals, the curriculum itself and the materials used also change.

In addition to that, standards have a tendency to break down because they measure something that is not necessarily rated in the same way at any given time. Perhaps the contents of a test or its outward form have influenced the way the subject has been taught. For example, the Danish spelling test after grade 9 was altered in 1978. The spelling primers which came out in the next decade clearly reflected this change. At the same time, the use of a spelling dictionary in connection with these tests was not only permitted, but became a matter of course. Sales of the authorised spelling dictionary increased at a great rate, and a positive change came about in the educational system. Learning of spelling by rote became less predominant and pupils were now more frequently taught how to use dictionaries to spell correctly.

If the test is to form part of the instruction, an educational-psychological analysis of possible and actual results is necessary.

Among other things, it is important educationally to make the pupils feel like setting to work and solving the tasks of the test. This is also desirable from a psychological point of view, when the aim is to measure at an optimal level and describe competence on that basis. Much so-called 'outward motivation' can be created through an educationally optimal presentation of a test.

On the other hand, so-called 'uninteresting material' may also reveal something about a pupil's reading behaviour. It is possible, of course, that the pupil's reading has become so automatic that he or she is able to master many different reading techniques and can process information without difficulty, even if the text is both difficult and utterly unimportant. Such tests can be used to good effect, especially by a competent tester.

It is important that test material should be lively and up to date. If tests are outdated they block development of their teaching materials. Nor, too, should tests used as research tools remain unchanged decade after decade; the use of contemporary educational-statistical methods enable us to standardise tests which were developed at different times and which have not been applied from the beginning of the sequence of testing (Allerup, 1984; 1985; 1986; Allerup and Sorber, 1977; Allerup et al, 1977).

Tests can 'prove' that the school is improving
Some people are of the opinion that when test scores improve, the *school* has improved. This is certainly not always so. It depends on what is being measured.

No doubt everyone is able to give an example of a long term constructive development of tests which can be used in everyday teaching (Nielsen et al, 1986a; 1986b; Soegard et al, 1983a; 1983b).

However, even very clear test results may present difficulties in their explanation. As an example: 'What is at the bottom of a rising test score?'. One survey (Jansen et al, 1987) showed a generally increasing reading competence over a number of years. But why? At the same time results indicated that even if today it were possible - through tests - to determine (part of) the educational needs of a pupil, for instance for special education, there are not always sufficient means available to meet such needs.

In such cases, the use of tests is often criticised - and, in my view, wrongly. It may be that a precise diagnosis can be made by means of a test. It is not the fault of the test that we cannot draw educationally appropriate consequences from that diagnosis.

Also much other criticism of tests is too facile, and critics fail to discriminate between the types of tests involved. People with different attitudes to tests often talk at cross-purposes.

TESTS, CRITICALLY ASSESSED
Tests take time
An aspect which is often overlooked in connection with tests is that *time* is a precious commodity - it can only be used once. And if tests do not make a valuable educational contribution, then they are a *waste of teaching time*.

Florander and Jansen calculated the time spent from the 2nd to the 9th year of school on a whole series of streaming tests in grade 5 and at the annual 'examinations' at the end of the school year (Florander & Jansen, 1966a; 1966b; 1966c; 1967; 1968; Nielsen, 1968; Florander, 1981). All in all, in

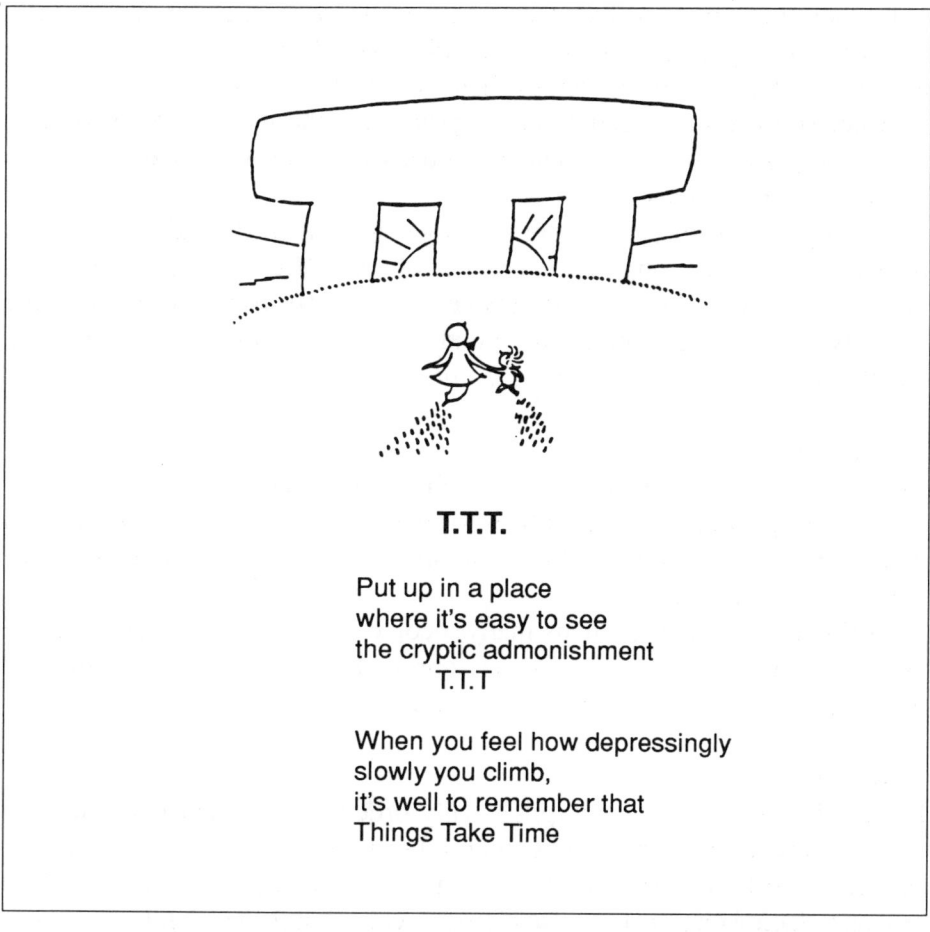

T.T.T.

Put up in a place
where it's easy to see
the cryptic admonishment
T.T.T

When you feel how depressingly
slowly you climb,
it's well to remember that
Things Take Time

seven years of schooling, the time spent on annual examinations, streaming tests and leaving examinations (not including individual examinations of separate schools) was equivalent to an entire school year. Twenty years later there is a general consensus that these tests were a waste of time.

Tests may convey a false sense of confidence.
Tests are also negative, if they mislead pupils and parents into thinking that 'Things are going well in school!'. It is possible that the results of some tests are even mistakenly taken to imply that 'The children are having a good time in school'. This is a much too simplified conclusion, and not generalisable. In addition, the results of a few tests are often taken for results covering a complete area of skills; this is in many cases unwarranted.

Furthermore, tests may result in a situation where some children constantly receive a message like 'Peter has difficulties in reading'. This is seldom news to these children and their parents (if it is true at all). Varied evaluations might have been more useful, but not a message based on the attainment of subskills, a summary of corrected work and a number which is perhaps converted into an even more summary mark.

When this happens, pupils are no longer motivated to read 'because the books are fun or exciting' but in order to obtain a 'Beta Plus', and A/B or a 9.3' - or whatever the local marking system is currently using. Tests contribute towards shaping the motivation behind reading; and the *set reading task*, which may be formal or informal, is often changed through such a test.

Tests are a measure of prestige
Moreover, a negative feature of tests is that sometimes they become a sort of 'measure of prestige': pupils with high scores not only estimate their own and their peers' skill, but also attach importance to the order of precedence indicated by the tests.

At this point, some, perhaps many, people would view this competitive aspect positively, and make comparisons with developments in sport and politics, or even with the circus ring. I do not agree.

Misuse of test results?
If a teacher recognises the pupils' 'daily order of precedence' in the total results of the test ('Karen is better than John; John is better than Tina'), he or she reinforces his or her existing views of the competence of the pupils. Their separate placing on a scale is in agreement with what the teacher knew before the test.

It may be the case that the teacher expects the results of a reading test (which can be about the reading of isolated words and perhaps de-coding of pictures) to be the same as ability in the daily reading of whole books or other connected texts.

However, it would be more reasonable to expect that results (from a very simple test) that put the pupils into an order of precedence would be different from the more 'whole results' which the teacher sees every day. If the teacher only heeds the results of the test, a full knowledge of, for example, the pupils' reading ability, will not be obtained.

Another inappropriate use of tests is seen in cases when on the basis of an unexpected order of precedence of the pupils (that is, when there is a discrepancy between the test results and the teacher's expectations) the teacher rejects the systematised description as irrelevant: 'A sensible and practical understanding of the pupil's daily reading shows that the pupil is a good reader'.

The teacher may be caught on the horns of a dilemma of having to decide whether 'the test is superfluous', or 'judgment based on daily observation of the pupil is wrong', or 'the test is lying'. However, a pupil who gets on very well in class may be a poor reader according to a specific test. And this discovery could mean that the pupil was tested specifically in the skills he or she did not master, rather than in 'reading' in general.

It goes without saying that a teacher may go from 'misuse' to 'appropriate use' of test results by looking into what the test is testing, comparing this with evidence from day-to-day observation of the child, and then working with the pupil, making adaptations in teaching by choosing appropriate subject area activities and reading materials.

'When the test says one thing, and day-to-day experience says something else, even trained teachers must have the courage to trust their own judgment'. This is how Thomas Sigsgaard, a Danish psychologist, began his lectures about the use of tests at the University of Copenhagen in the 1950s. This maxim is still worth remembering.

Tests are no better than the people who ought to bring them up to date
In their review of Danish reading tests (1980), of which they had an essentially positive opinion, Soegard and Hansen found that 'a considerable number of the current tests (especially tests published by central institutions) were devised according to the theoretical foundations of the 1920s or 1930s, designed in the 1930s or 1940s, and constructed in the 1940s and 1950s. They were usable at that time, but became obsolete by the 1960s and 1970s. However, they are still being used today when we are approaching the 1990s, long after the prior conditions, on the basis of which they were worked out, have changed radically.'

This criticism probably applies in general to countries with weakly developed test systems.

Many things are not measured
Too great a reliance on tests can mean that the definition of education is narrowed down to what is measurable.

In his effort to make science exact, Galileo said 'Measure everything that can be measured, and make the immeasurable measurable'. It is difficult to object to this clear wording, especially if there is general agreement about what is immeasurable in a given situation. However, there is a risk that the wording will further an education which happens to overrate what *can* be measured at a given time. And then the emphasis of the education swings towards what is measurable *now*. This can be unwise. Therefore, *the scientist Piet Hein (1963), suggests this addition to the above maxim: 'And do not attach more importance to what can be measured at a given time than to what happens to be immeasurable.'

We cannot do without exact measuring, when what is measured is exactly measurable. *However, we must be aware of what is not measured;* this applies particularly to reading, perhaps also to much other teaching. The smaller the parts which are measured, the greater the certainty with which we measure - and the more unimportant the result may prove to be.

It is almost tempting to quote E E Cummings: 'While you and I have lips and voices / which are for kissing and to sing with / who cares if some one-eyed son of a bitch / invents an instrument to measure spring with?' (quoted in Poplin, 1986).

When the tests get the blame

Not infrequently, tests have been cast in the role of whipping-boy, when the real problem was that it was never really clear why tests were necessary in the first place.

For example, there has been much debate in Denmark about the tests used to determine whether children are ready to begin formal schooling. Opinions adverse to, and in defence of, the testing were voiced, but the purpose of the test became clear only when an understanding of the concept of 'school preparedness' was achieved. Thomsen (1957) described it as follows:

> To be prepared for school largely means that in a number of non- clarified areas there must be certain, mainly unknown, necessary prior conditions so that children at the age of 5, 6 and 7 are able to start their schooling with a fair chance of success, at some school or other among the multitude of schools, with the current curriculum plan of the school concerned, and to live up to exactly those ways and methods of beginning instruction and other treatment which are employed by the teacher with whom they happen to be placed.

Tests also get the blame when 'Silent Spring' is mentioned, not Rachel Carson's 'Silent Spring' (1963) which was such a pronounced starting point for the environmental debate, but another 'environmental debate': the fact that

---

* I have used 'scientist' here instead of 'natural scientist' as there is no clear distinction in English between the German Wissenschafther and Naturwissentchafther. Wissenschaft is a hard concept to translate into English.

human beings, at the age when they are mostly absorbed in themselves and in friends of their own age, have to spend two of the most delightful months of the year, not being interested in each other, but being interested in textbooks. The subject has mainly (and rightly) occupied writers of fiction.

However, when as adults they attack 'The Neglected Spring' (this is the title of a Danish book of fiction about the defects in the educational system, Scherfig, 1940), they forget that the reason for the misery is not the tests, but the educational system. Still, the tests almost always get the blame (Rasborg & Florander, 1966a; 1966b; 1967a; 1967b; Marckmann, 1966).

Tests: a negative assessment
In Denmark in the 1970s, educational (and psychological) tests in general were viewed almost entirely negatively. They were regarded as tools of the oppressive structure of society, and consequently they had to be laid aside. Come the revolution, tests were to be dispensed with entirely. (Jensen, 1970; Kryger, 1975). Testing was seen as superfluous, harmful and all forms of 'labelling' were rejected. The connection to reality was cut.

For the theorists of the 70s, this workshop would be meaningful only if it agreed to abolish all tests and exclude formalised evaluation of all kinds. The picture in America at the time was similar. Boyer (1974) described 'the American test madness, sorting children like potatoes'. I have seen no evidence of this madness in Scandinavia.

A constructive approach to testing
Mainly during the first decades of the 20th century some people expected that it would be possible, via tests, to obtain precise, meaningful and clear measurements of the acquisition of a skill within the area of education. This was just as naive as the views put forward by those concerned with the abolition of tests in the 70s.

Some of the classical yearly surveys describe a development in the view of tests, eg the surveys by Buros, 1978; 1983; Anastasi, 1988; Fischer, 1974; cf. also for instance Educational Testing Service's many publications. Other examples will no doubt be put forward by participants.

Cronbach is an example of a test psychologist who has neither a specifically positive, nor a specifically negative, but an analytic view of tests. He states, 1984:

> To be sure, testing serves conservative forces: it was military testing in World War 1 that first brought testing into prominence, and

employment managers, schools, and mental hospitals use tests to keep their institutions going smoothly. But do not be misled by the fact that the largest sales of tests are for essentially conservative purposes. Tests can also serve — indeed, are sometimes of great value to — the reformer. The pioneering tests of Galton, a hundred years ago, were inspired by, and did much to advance, the idea that a man's place should depend on what he can do and not on the social position of his parents. Precisely the same philosophy animates the pioneers, not too different from Miss Kimball, who are trying to provide disadvantaged children with fitting educational activities. Tests have been used in recent years to document the extent to which the schools fail the Negro. Tests have also demonstrated that a near-fascist personality can be found in many a person the community calls well-adjusted and successful (Adorno *et al,* 1950). Tests are neutral; they serve those who want to maintain society without change, and they are a weapon available to those who want to criticize present institutions and create a society based fully on merit and self-determination.

PRE-COMPREHENSION: AN UNNOTICED FACET?

Farr (1986) noted that in much evaluation, what 'ought to be the issue' was forgotten, and those involved rarely asked themselves 'What do I want to know about these children and about their reading competence?' In his view, we must consider their pre-comprehension (ie, 'the comprehension reserve' or the background knowledge of the individual pupil).

The more the individual pupil knows *beforehand* about the subject of a reading test, the better he is able to attempt it (Jansen, 1987; 1988).

This subject, viz. the pre-comprehension itself and the question of making it a focus of attention, is central to much debate about evaluation, at least in reading. The roots of functional illiteracy lie in the lack of pre-comprehension, and in most cases pre-comprehension contributes greatly towards determining educational patterns for the rest of the life.

Figure 2 illustrates an important aspect of the discussion about using tests to measure performance and the importance of pre-comprehension.

There are probably no longer any schools which work on the assumption that a test provides information which is then poured into the pupils who are supposed to get wiser *pari passu.* Pupils are not vessels to pour something into; they choose for themselves what they want to take from the information in a text which is *then* processed into knowledge in some form.

Figure 2
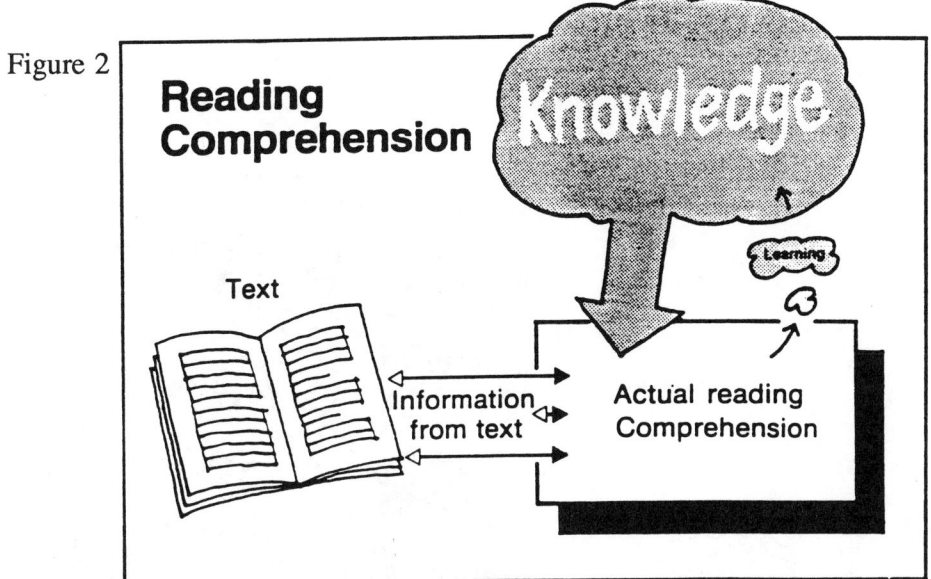

In Figure 2 there are arrows pointing from text to person; they indicate that information can be taken up. But there are also arrows pointing from person to text, since the pieces of information must be *collected* in order to be processed into knowledge in the individual. When this takes place, the background knowledge of the person increases, and a two-way process has been set in motion.

Figure 3 indicates that the pre-comprehension of the children determines which of the different pieces of information they accept and incorporate into their own knowledge structures.

At this point it is important to make clear that the cognitive ingredients within the person are elements which do not exist in isolation. To a much higher degree than many teachers of Danish traditionally imagine, emotional and social factors are also in the picture all the time.

The problem is NOT the evaluation, and NOT the tests
A Danish lay preacher was asked, at the beginning of the 20th century, whether card-playing was a sin. He replied that 'as far as he knew, the Jack of Clubs had never done any harm, but he was often seen in bad company'.

Figure 3

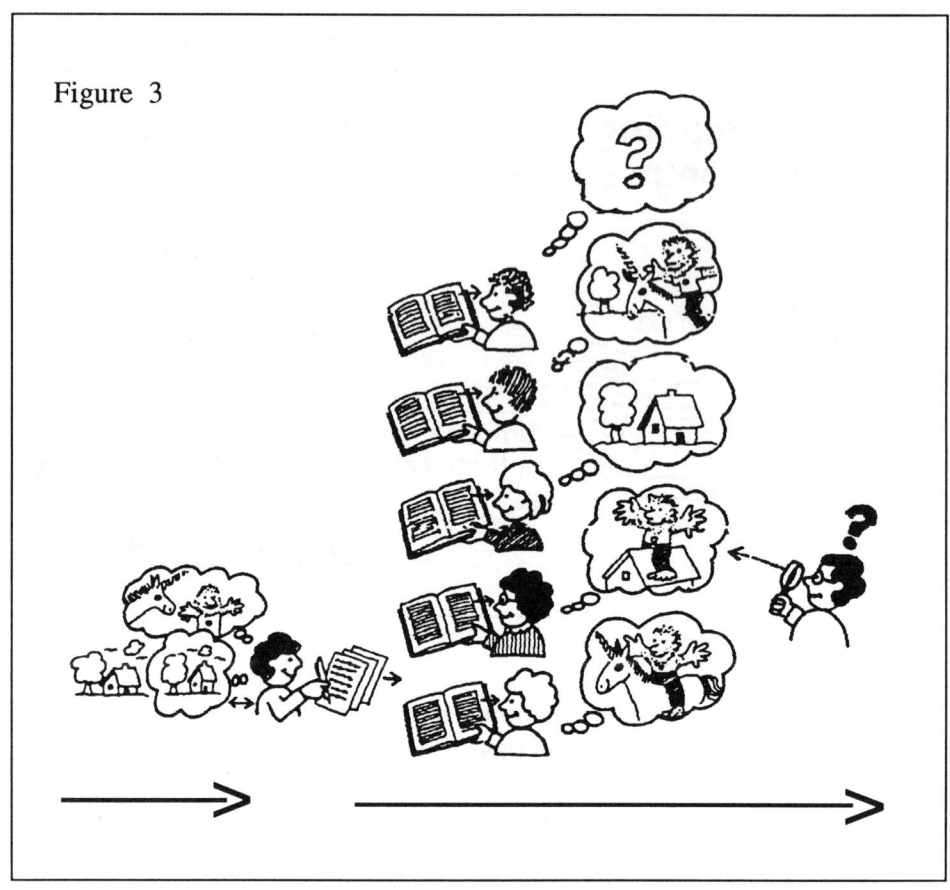

Evaluation is not a sin either. Tests do not make mischief of their own accord. The problem is that *we* use evaluation in areas where it makes no sense to do so, and that *we* content ourselves with a test which is not good enough for the purpose; in that case,*we* are the problem.

We might use date-stamping and informative labels
Tests might be date-stamped to indicate that they had 'a limited shelf life' and should not be used after the date on the cover. That would warn pupils, parents, teachers, school administrators and politicians, and would guard against there being tests which provided irrelevant data, because they rested on an erroneous foundation. Perhaps we ought also to extend the informative labels so that certain tests are applied only under quite specific circumstances. And the interpretation ought to be carried out by competent educationists who not only know the tests, but have a solid knowledge of the individual pupils tested.

An alternative to tests?
In the longer term we should devise other means of evaluation and not rely solely on tests. It is possible that these methods would replace tests entirely or, alternatively, be used in conjunction with existing teaching methods.

The better the contact with the child's home environment, the less the school's need for tests. The more adept the teacher at observing pupils, the less necessary the tests. The teacher who has few pupils in the class (eg 14-18 pupils) has a better background for evaluating them than the teacher who has many pupils, perhaps 28-38. In schools where pupils have the same teacher for several consecutive years, there is no need for routine tests.

However, perhaps considerations like these are beyond the scope of this conference? My private wish is that evaluation was a modest, but natural part of daily life in school, and that tests would on occasion, but rarely, form part of the evaluation process. Tests would still be used for research purposes and in cases where pupils with different types of handicap need to be helped by means of special diagnostic techniques. Furthermore, the tests ought to measure what we expect to need in 15-30 years. Perhaps we should expect that the objective of society at that time will be to place human beings permanently on the moon or on the planet Mars? Perhaps the objective will be more humble, for example, to find out what killer whales tell each other, to secure time and encouragement for everybody to work, row on the lake, read Old Greek, play football, speak with other human beings? In any case, the evaluative procedures which are being established must be anchored in a future about which we know nothing, but have to take seriously - so seriously that we have to develop our evaluation techniques in the light of this future.

References
ALLERUP, Peter (1984) Analyses of development curves by means of Rasch models. In: MORTENSEN, L. Spange (ed) *Symposium of Applied Statistics, Aarhus, January 25-27, 1984.* Copenhagen: NEUCC, RECAU, RECKU, pp 183—196, 20.

ALLERUP, Peter (1985) *Why I Like to Read — a statistical analysis of questionnaire data.* Copenhagen: The Danish Institute for Educational Research, 61.

ALLERUP, Peter (1986) *Statistical analysis of MADRS — a rating scale.* Copenhagen: The Danish Institute for Educational Research, 61.

ALLERUP, Peter, MYLOV, Peer *and* SPELLING, Soren (1977) *Developmental Curves through Item Analysis.* Copenhagen: The Danish Institute for Educational Research, 41.

ALLERUP, Peter *and* SORBER, Gordon (1977) *The Rasch Model for Questionnaires with a Computer Program.* Second revised edition. Copenhagen: The Danish Institute for Educational Research, 4.

ANASTASI, Anne (1988) *Psychological Testing.* 6th ed New York: The Macmillan Company.

BOYER, Gil: Quoted In: JANSEN, M. (1974) *Tendencies in the Educational development?* Copenhagen: The Danish Institute of Educational Research.

BUROS, Oscar Krisen (ed) (1983) *The Eighth Mental Measurements Yearbook.* Vol I. Highland Park, N. J.: The Gryphon Press, 1978.

BUROS, Oscar Krisen (ed) (1983) *Tests in Print.* 3rd ed. Highland Park, N. J.: The Gryphon Press.

CARSON, Rachel (1963) *Det Tavse Forar* (The Silent Spring). Copenhagen: Gyldendal.

CHALL, Jeanne S. (1967) *Learning to Read: the great debate.* New York: McGraw Hill, Inc.

CRONBACH, Lee J. (1984) *Essentials of Psychological Testing.* 4th ed. New York: Harper & Row.

THE DANISH LANGUAGE COUNCIL (1986) *Dictionary of Spelling.* Copenhagen: Gyldendal.

FARR, Roger C. (1986) *Research and Development in the Assessment of Reading Comprehension.* London: Eleventh World Congress on Reading, July 30.

FISCHER, Gerhard H. (1974) *Einführung in die Theorie Psychologischer Tests* [Introduction to the Theory of Psycholgical Tests]. Bern: Verlag Hans Huber.

FLORANDER, Jesper (1981) Our evaluation of one another — a phenomenon which will remain, *Folkeskolen,* 98, (50/51) 1878—1880.

FLORANDER, Jesper and JANSEN, Mogens (1966a) Examination, annual examinations, and waste of time, *Folkeskolen,* 83 (20) 972—973 and 991—993.

FLORANDER, Jesper and JANSEN, Mogens (1966b) Examination madness or examination for the sake of the examinations, *Folkeskolen,* 83 (21) 1040—1042.

FLORANDER, Jesper and JANSEN, Mogens (1966c) Examination madness and the value of the examination, *Folkeskolen,* 83 (32/33) 1412—1414.

FLORANDER, Jesper and JANSEN, Mogens (1967) Why do we examine — and why do we not use streaming? *Folkeskolen,* 84 (1) 8 —10.

FLORANDER, Jesper and JANSEN, Mogens (1968) About the value of annual examinations, *The Municipal School of Copenhagen,* 61 (36) 689.

HEIN, Piet (1963) *Kilden og Krukken.* Fabler og Essays. [The Fountain and the Jar. Fables and Essays]. Copenhagen: Gyldendale.

JANSEN, Mogens (1966) *Skriftligt arbejde i dansk . 1—7* skoleår. [Written activities in Danish Grades 1—7]. Registration and analysis of books for the mother tongue instruction in Danish. Copenhagen: The Danish Institute for Educational Research, 60.

JANSEN, Mogens (1969) *Danske læsebøger 1— 7 skoleår.* [Danish Readers, Grades 1 — 7]. Vol. I: Registration and analysis. Vol II: Register of writers and titles. Copenhagen: The Danish Institute for Educational Research, 70.

JANSEN, Mogens (1975) *Teaching of Foreign Language and Mother Tongue — examined through an empiric investigation of Danish teaching in Iceland through classroom observations.* The statistical analysis in Vol II in co-operation with Svend Kreinder Møller. Copenhagen: Munksgaard, 79.

JANSEN, Mogens (1984) Ulven kommer IKKE! [The wolf is NOT coming!]. *Læsepædagogen* [The Reading Teacher], 32 (1) 1 - 2.

JANSEN, Mogens (1987) Fremtidens fagbog — og de læsehandicappede [The future book of non-fiction—and the disabled readers], *Læsepædagogen* [The Reading Teacher] 35 (8) 315 - 326. Offprint.

JANSEN, Mogens (1988) Hvorfor kan vi ikke læse fagtekster? [Why can't we read subject material?] *Sprog & Samfund*, 6 (1) 3 - 7. Offprint.

JANSEN, Mogens *and* AHM, Jette (1971) *Arbejdsbøger til dansk, børnehaveklassen og 1 — 7 skoleår.* [Workbooks for the teaching of Danish. Kindergarten class and Grades 1 — 7]. Registration and analysis. Copenhagen: The Danish Institute for Educational Research, No 72, issued by The Danish Library Bureau.

JANSEN, Mogens, KREINER, Svend, KROGH, Tove *and* NIELSEN, Henning W. (1987) *Sproglige forudsætninger og senere skolegangsresultater* [Linguistic qualifications and later achievements in school]. Copenhagen: Søllerød kommune/Forlaget Skolepsykologi/[The Danish Institute for Educational Research], Den blå serie nr 10 [The Blue Series, 10].

JENSEN, Jesper (1970) Psykologens roller i samfundet. [The roles of the psychologist in the society]. *Nordisk Psykologi,* 22, 41 - 53.

KREINER, Svend (1986) *Statistisk Analyse af Klasserumsobservationer* [Statistical analysis of classroom observations]. Copenhagen: The Danish Institute for Education Research.

KRYGER, Niels (1975) Enhedsskolens tabere [The losers of the comprehensive school]. In: GLÆSEL, B. (ed) *Kan vi Undvære Specialundervisningen?* [Could we do without the special education?]. Copenhagen: Gyldendals Pædagogiske Bibliotek pp 60 — 90.

MARCKMANN, Wilhelm (1966) Nogle erfaringer fra brugen af Uppsalaprøven [Some experiences from the use of the Uppsala Test]. Dansk Pædagogisk Tidsskrift, 14 (7) 316 — 331.

NIELSEN, Jørgen Chr., KREINER, Svend, POULSEN, Anders *and* SØEGÅRD, Arne (1986a) *Sætningslæseprøven SL 40* [Sentence Reading Test SL 40]. Copenhagen: Dansk Psykologisk Forlag.

NIELSEN, Jørgen Chr., KREINER, Svend, POULSEN, Anders *and* SØEGÅRD, Arne (1986b) *Sætningslæseprøven SL 60* [Sentence Reading Test SL 60]. Copenhagen: Dansk Psykologisk Forlag.

NIELSEN, Sv. Aa., (1968) Om vores årsprøvers værdi [About the value of our annual examinations], *The Municipal School of Copenhagen,* 61 (35) 670 - 672.

POPLIN, Mary (1986) The Quest for Meaning. In: DOUGLASS, M. P. (ed) *Claremont Reading Conference.* Claremont, Cal.: The Claremont Reading Conference, pp 1 - 27.

RASBORG, Finn *and* FLORANDER, Jesper (1966a) Uppsalaprøvens prognostiske værdi. [The prognostic value of the Uppsala Test], *Skolepsykologi,* 3 (2) 67 - 73.

RASBORG, Finn *and* FLORANDER, Jesper (1966b) Uppsalaprøvens. Kommentar til Bording Petersens indlæg [The Uppsala Test. Comments on the presentation by Bording Petersen]. *Skolepsykologi,* 3, 4, 184 - 187.

RASBORG, Finn *and* FLORANDER, Jesper (1967a) *Om Uppsalaprøvens prognostiske værdi* [About the prognostic value of the Uppsala Test]. Copenhagen: The Danish Institute for Educational Research.

RASBORG, Finn *and* FLORANDER, Jesper (1967b) Pædagogisk skolestart. Med eller uden Uppsalaprøvepoints? [Educational school beginning. With or without Uppsala Test scores?]. *Dansk Pædagogisk Tidsskrift,* 15 (7) 294 — 304.

SCHERFIG, Hans (1940) *Det Forsømte Forår* [The Neglected Spring]. Copenhagen: Gyldendal.

SØEGÅRD, Arne *and* HANSEN, Mogens (1980) *Læsetests* [Reading Tests]. *Helsingør: Forlaget Skolepsykologi.* Den røde serie nr. 9 [The Red Series, No 9].

SØEGÅRD, Arne, HESSELHOLDT, Svend, KREINER, Svend, NIELSEN, Jørgen Chr., POULSEN, Anders *and* SPELLING, Søren (1983a) *Ordstillelæsningsprøven OS 64* [Word Silent Reading Test OS 64]. Copenhagen: Dansk Psykologisk Forlag.

SØEGÅRD, Arne, HESSELHOLDT, Svend, KREINER, Svend, NIELSEN, Jørgen Chr., POULSEN, Anders *and* SPELLING, Søren (1983b) *Ordstillelæsningsprøven* OS 120 [Word Silent Reading Test OS 120]. Copenhagen: Dansk Psykologisk Forlag.

THOMSEN, Erik (1957) Nogle problemer ved vurdering og karaktergivning [Some problems in connection with evaluation and marking], *Dansk Pædagogisk Tidsskrift,* 5, (9) 385 - 405.

3
Evaluation and the Reform of Schools

Helen Simons
The Institute of Education
University of London, England

The current reform proposals will fail, as they have in the past, because they attempt to reform education simply by telling teachers (and everyone else) what to do, rather than by empowering them to do what must be done.

Murray, 1986, p 29[1]

As it happens, this comment comes from the USA. Its aptness to the United Kingdom, however, is more than a coincidence. It reflects a general trend in Western democracies towards greater control and specification of school work as a means of improving the efficiency and effectiveness of the service schools provide. The Education Act of 1988, which now constitutes the legislative framework for schooling in England and Wales, embodies radically new arrangements for the government of schools. Teachers are indeed to be told what to do and parents invited to judge their worth on the basis of competitive performance. The curriculum will be prescribed, pupil achievement assessed and made public as the basis for consumer evaluation. At this point in time it is not clear, at least to me, whether the corresponding legislation now in preparation for Scottish schools will mirror or hopefully soften these arrangements. I say 'hopefully' because nothing I have to say in this paper supports the government's view of how to improve schools, or indeed of how to generate and use evaluation data in the context of such an aim.

I will begin with a brief review of what evaluators have learned from thirty years of monitoring various forms of central intervention in the conduct of schooling. I shall conclude by arguing the case for a model of school improvement based on professional self-direction and professional accountability. In the course of the paper I hope to demonstrate how evaluation, both as a theory and as a practice, has evolved from technicist beginnings to an educative process with a key role to play in this alternative scenario. I am keenly aware, as I do so, that this scenario may well have to await more propitious times before it can be fully realised. It is a long-term view of change.

DEVELOPMENTS IN EVALUATION THINKING

In focusing attention exclusively on student acquisition of pre-specified learning objectives the government has now enshrined in legislation a view of evaluation that even in the sixties was already giving way to a more sophisticated appreciation of information needs in relation to curriculum development. As the problems of change, and particularly of resistance to change, revealed themselves to would-be innovators and evaluators alike as a complex set of interlocking but poorly understood phenomena, attention to the rather barren field of measurable learning outcomes rapidly waned. In its place evaluators, encouraged at least in the early stages by puzzled administrators and sponsors of innovations, extended their field of vision to include the processes and contexts of implementation, seeking better understandings of what had gone wrong and a better basis for more effective strategies of intervention. This shift of focus had a number of highly significant consequences in the form of concomitant changes in the theory and practice of evaluation.[2]

In the first place evaluators began to see themselves less in the role of providing formative feedback to curriculum development teams, enabling these teams to improve their products and tactics, and more in the role of providing an information service to decision-makers, among whom the curriculum development teams constituted only one group, and a very temporary group at that. In the second place, the methodology changed to encompass the ever-expanding matrix of information requirements. The early seventies, a period of prolific inventiveness, saw the rise of a new language of evaluation as the objectivist thinking of conventional psychological research gave way to subjectivist epistemologies designed to guide and legitimate the much more broad-ranging inquiries upon which evaluators were embarking. These new approaches, termed variously responsive, illuminative, transactional, holistic, were more sociological than psychological in relation to disciplinary traditions, though the imperative of action-relevance involved the evaluators in drawing from multiple sources in an effort to marry their efforts to the vocabularies of action they were attempting to serve within severe time and resource constraints. The case study emerged as a vehicle capable of integrating the increasingly diverse information dimensions of the situation analysis that confronted programme evaluators, and the narrative form, invoking further complications through association with artistic and particularly literary traditions, also began to feature prominently in evaluation reports. The generic term that came to be adopted as an umbrella for all these new approaches was the term 'naturalistic'.[3]

But the methodological shift brought in its train an even more important change in the evaluation perspective. Moving 'beyond the numbers game' into the study of people, institutions and policies forced evaluators to confront the political nature of their role, an awareness sharpened in the seventies by a tendency on the part of central agencies to adopt more coercive strategies in the search for curriculum change that was becoming increasingly prescriptive. In 1974 MacDonald introduced the concept of democratic evaluation[4], crystallising the emerging unease about the role of the evaluator in the redistribution of power, and calling for evaluation to be more consistent with the professed values of the liberal democratic state. His central proposal, that the evaluator act as a broker in the trading of information between the powerful and the powerless, placed a responsibility on the evaluator to adopt methods of generating and reporting information that were easily understood and widely accessible, thus widening further the gap between social science orthodoxy and evaluation practice.

At this conference I have been asked to deal specifically with how to do evaluation. I hope I have already made it clear in the account so far that methodology is much more than a set of technical options that can be discussed in isolation from considerations of the social purposes, uses and consequences of evaluation. If evaluation is, as I believe it important to be, a political activity, then the methodology of evaluation is bound to be circumscribed by political considerations. Speaking for myself, and speaking primarily as an educationist with a special interest in evaluation, I must also add that the methodology of evaluation must, for me, be consistent with educational intent. For me education and politics are mutually constitutive. I take education to be about the empowerment through self-knowledge of individuals, politics to be about the empowerment through social knowledge of social groups. In the practice of evaluation these views of education and politics can become intimately intertwined. MacDonald, for instance, writes of an approach to participants in a case study evaluation which comes close to embodying such an aspiration:

> When we are negotiating access to the people in the case... let us say to them that we assume all social action is a compromise of some kind between values, interests and circumstances, and that our task, and theirs, is not to defend or attack that compromise, but to understand its precise structure. This is not a promise, but an invitation to locate the evaluative act where the action is.
>
> MacDonald, 1981, p 6

Although, in this paper I go on to talk primarily about school evaluation, this 'invitation' is not restricted to teachers, or to pupils and parents. It is applicable at all levels of social action. That such an aspiration has methodological implications is undeniable, as will be apparent from what follows. But I want to begin by turning now to my own experience of evaluating schools as a basis for constructing the scenario I mentioned at the beginning.

Learning from experience
It was in conducting external case studies of schools engaged in central curriculum reform, and especially in adopting a democratic approach, that I came to realise the potential of school self-evaluation for improvement. My conclusions were firstly that the school should be the basic unit of change; secondly that the teachers should be centrally involved in creating the change; and thirdly that the management and structure of the school needed to change if they were not severely to limit the possibility of changing anything else within it.

Before examining the school self-evaluation thesis more closely, let me try to summarise the essential elements in change theory as they came to be understood through evaluation of the curriculum reform movement:

1. There can be no curriculum development without teacher development. This was a very early recognition in the Humanities Curriculum Project that came to be embodied in the teacher-as-researcher concept and the action-research movement that subsequently developed from it.[6]

2. Teachers cannot break through and sustain new practice without support at the institutional and local advisory level. This is obvious now, perhaps, but many curriculum projects had assumed that they could work directly and exclusively with individual classroom teachers. Change is a professional community activity.

3   Power-coercive strategies of change gain surface adoption but fail to affect basic attitudes. They are, moreover, likely to fuel resistance to change. Innovations that are not challenging are easily adopted; those which embody fundamental change are difficult to implement and are frequently rejected.

4   Schools as Whitehead (1932) observed long ago need to be understood in their particular circumstances and with regard to their local clientele. Prescriptions of curricular action should not supplant the judgments of those who have to implement them.

5   No change effort is likely to be successful unless those responsible for its success have a sense of ownership of the change.

6   There can be no significant teacher development, and therefore no curriculum change, without institutional change. Institutional values act to frustrate, limit and neutralise teacher development.

7   Any desired outcome has to be considered within a time-scale of at least ten years and a framework of system, institutional and in-service support to effect that change.

8   Neither the freemarket strategy (the rationale of curriculum development in the 1960s) nor command/compliance (the rationale of curriculum development more characteristic of the 1970s and 1980s) appear to yield the kind of curriculum change that is sought. We should think, rather, in terms of educational communities of professionals and their constituencies working together in a spirit of shared responsibility and mutual accountability.

The theory of school development which underlies this approach to the evaluation of change is one that is primarily democratic in intent; it is based upon the key values of community, diversity and relationships of mutual accountability. It assumes, furthermore, that in the conduct and dissemination of evaluation, fairness, reasonableness and respect for persons must be guiding values, anything less inimical to it. I will return to this focus at the end of the paper in examining the way forward.

Learning from abroad
If we take a look at the United States, we can note a similar pattern. House (1980) was one of the first to highlight the deficiencies of the curriculum

reform movement. In his paper *Technology Versus Craft: a ten year perspective on innovation,* he distinguishes three perspectives on innovation: technological - a rational, hierarchical, consensus-model to which he ascribes much of the reform effort of the sixties utilising an RD&D (Research, Development and Diffusion) model; political - that takes account of the inevitable conflicts of values and goals that are likely to accompany any major innovation and that involve negotiation with different interest groups, compromise and mutual adaption; and cultural - an approach to innovation that has to interact with and be open to be shaped by the communities of individuals in schools and local districts that are supposed to be affected by the change. Smith has recently summarised the shift of focus thus: 'Overall, House sees the shift moving from the innovation *per se*, to the innovation in context, to the context *per se*.' (Smith et al, 1987, p285).

The approach to evaluation suggested in the next section of this paper is an interaction of these last two perspectives. Despite these and other analyses of what went wrong with curriculum reform efforts of the sixties, a new wave of state reforms has swept the US since the publication in 1983 of *A Nation at Risk.* While this new wave of reform had a different origin, being more politically motivated, the solutions, comments Sizer (1988) were modest and unchallenging, geared towards improving the minimal status of teachers and minimal improvement of test scores. 'State reform activity', he concludes, 'has been remarkably conservative; the basic institutions are largely unchallenged.' (pxi)

And Timar and Kirp (1988) conclude from their study of three state reform efforts, that neither the rationalist strategy for improving schools nor the decentralist strategy is likely to lead to serious improvement in the quality of schooling in America, partly, they go on to argue, because the language of reform fails to encompass how teachers talk about reform and school improvement. But more than this: 'Reform is possible only if policy makers focus their attention to improving the organisational health of schools.'
(Timar and Kirp, 1988, p137)

School self-evaluation
In the mid-seventies in the UK and in many other parts of the world, a movement in school self-evaluation began to take shape. This movement was a reaction to many factors (economic, political, social and cultural), had several purposes (for accountability, managerial efficiency, professional development), and took a variety of forms (checklists for self-review,

organisational analysis and process-oriented, issue based work).[7] My own interest in this movement stemmed, as I have said, from the realisation in evaluating curriculum reforms, that an understanding of the culture of the school and of the role of the key protagonists in that culture was central to any change effort. Drawing on this experience I formulated an approach to school self-evaluation[8] that had the following features:

> the institution, not the individual teacher or student was the major unit of change; teacher development and pupil performance issues were considered in the context of whole school policies;

> the focus of evaluative efforts was cross-curricular policies; policies that affect all pupils and to which all teachers have a commitment;

> the utilisation of 'low technology', techniques and methods such as interviewing, observation, documentary analysis, questionnaires, that were familiar to teachers in the context of teaching and could be adapted for the purposes of evaluating;

> the adoption of a collaborative and participative ethic involving as many teachers as possible in the process, though not all perhaps at the one time;

> the institution of forms of organisation that ensured the process was built into the working structure of the school.

The emphasis on the school as a whole does not mean a neglect of evaluation of teacher performance or pupil achievement. On the contrary, it enables a more sensitive approach to be taken to these issues by considering them within the context of the shared aspirations of the institution. Nor does it mean that the school evaluates only for its own internal purposes. School self-evaluation certainly provides the basis for school development but also for volunteered public knowledge. Such an emphasis allows for a more comprehensive evaluation, one that is more sensitive to a range of affecting variables and more fair. It also, providing appropriate structures are built in for resolving conflicts of value in a non-threatening way, allows the school to tolerate increased uncertainty, to make more refined judgments about policy and practice and to have the confidence to respond more openly and effectively to external demands.

The main argument I have advanced for suggesting that schools engage in school self-evaluation is enhanced professionalism. It is important to be explicit about what this means for two reasons. First because it is often contrasted with evaluation of schools that is primarily managerial in intent; and secondly, because the rhetoric is frequently invoked to encourage adoption of schemes that are not open in fact to professional development.

The concept of professionalism I have in mind is intimately connected to the educative intent for evaluation I outlined earlier. I am committed to the view that self-direction by accountable professionals offers the best hope of continuous improvement in the educational experience offered to children by schools. Though teachers are the main protagonists in school self-evaluation as outlined in this paper, the concept applies equally to all those other professionals, administrators, advisers, curriculum officers, HMI, who have a role to play in improving the educational experience on offer to children. This concept of self-direction, though it seems to some like teacher protectionism, does not entail insulation against lay influences on what professionals do, or lay judgment of how well they do it. On the contrary, it presumes that professionals are accountable and not only to their pupils and colleagues, but to the community they serve as well - that they are committed to mediating a community brief in terms of the educational needs of particular children. There is, then, a proper relationship between accountability and professionalism; it is the terms on which this is proposed, to whom and for what one is precisely accountable that is the crux of the issue and needs to be mediated.

Self-accountable professionals do not only reflect upon their practice to improve the internal working of the school. They evaluate what they do against self-generated critical standards, they research shortfalls in provision and performance, they respond to changes of context and clientele, they experiment, they develop new programmes to solve identified problems, they collaborate, they engage in persuasive negotiation with the constituencies whose support and approval they need. (see House and Lapan, 1988, Hoyle, 1975, Wise et al, 1984, for other definitions). It is a responsive community-based professionalism, whether that community is a community of teachers within or between schools, or between schools and the local education authority, or between schools, their parents and the broader community. It provides the basis for the recognition that Reid (1987) believes professionals need:

> ...we should remind ourselves of the importance for professional practice of the support of publics outside the professions and beyond institutions ... the theory on which professions act gets its essential

meaning and significance from the outside world, not simply from the consensus of those within a profession. It is therefore essential that they address themselves to these wider publics to implant in their minds the image of the profession which those within it would like to own. (p14)

I have spent a little time exploring the concept of 'professionalism' because it is frequently invoked these days in relation to teacher appraisal, the national curriculum and other policy initiatives with little understanding of what is entailed by the concept and what support and resources are needed to secure it. It is the acceptable rhetoric, which nobody can deny, on which any reform proposal, it seems, can gain ready recognition that it is worth adopting.

Learning from the second wave of reform
We have now had more than a generation of experience of school self-evaluation as a major reform effort to begin to evaluate the effectiveness of this approach to the reform of schools. In an early review, Shipman in 1983 commented that the school self-evaluation movement was tending to repeat many of the mistakes of the curriculum development movement. These similarities he indicated referred to the many variations in school self-evaluation, whether LEA-initiated or teacher-initiated, though it was most obvious in the former and those projects like GRIDS[9] which primarily adopted the RD&D model which characterised many of the early curriculum reform projects. His analyses of the key weaknesses include the observations that evaluation was often adopted as an end in itself, not as a means to an end; that it was not conceived as a central part of school organisation, that it was piecemeal, not connected with whole curriculum analysis, that it was often prescriptive in intent (referring to many LEA checklists) and that many of the models available (LEA-initiated checklists[10] and GRIDS, for example,) did not embody a theory of change that related to the working of the school as a whole.

Five years later, of course, we have much more experience to draw on including learning to some extent from past mistakes. There is now much more awareness of the need to take account of whole school processes both at the management level and at the level of curriculum, teaching and learning processes, of the need to involve a large number of the school staff in the process of evaluating and, though to a lesser extent, of the need to build in structures to facilitate the process. To some extent this development has been facilitated by changes in in-service funding and LEA responses to inservice.[11]

Many local education authorities now require their schools, as a first stage in determining their INSET priorities, to submit an institutional development plan outlining the schools' own priorities for staff and school development. Sometimes, though not always, this is built upon an evaluation or self-review scheme. We wait to see whether the latest schemes for devolving financial management[12] to schools build upon the best of these developments or whether it becomes the prerogative of a few in the management hierarchy of the school.

My own experience in evaluating the efforts of schools to become self-determining reflexive communities has led to a number of observations about how we might improve this second stage of institutional self-evaluation. Early observations of the difficulties of many LEA-initiated systems were not dissimilar to those noted by Shipman (vide supra) (see Simons 1986). Then there was a set of factors related to the innovative nature of the task. It was clear that there had to be a total commitment by the school to the task, external support from the LEA, that teachers needed time to build a common commitment and language in which to talk about evaluation. It was clear also that systematic formal evaluation was more than a formalising of 'natural practice'; that there were other evaluation skills to be learnt. (Simons 1981). But beyond these rather obvious factors that might accompany many an innovative effort, there are three observations that are more directly related to an evaluation process that aspires to change schools.

The first is the need to create a culture of collaboration. In many schools this is not something that automatically exists. The process of school self-evaluation has to be built into the structure of the school and underpinned by forms of organisation that encourage participation by all staff and pupils, that demand collective deliberation of results, that allow conflicts of value to be confronted and resolved, that require, in other words, that the knowledge gained through the evaluation is utilised in action at the point of impact and is carried through by the majority of staff.

It should also be open to changes within the organisation of the school itself. Many of the early case studies of school self-evaluation efforts (see Clift et al, 1987, Shipman, 1983) indicated that the organisation of the evaluation mirrored that of the schools concerned, rather than created the conditions in which schools could generate their own basis for change. Elsewhere (see Simons, 1987, ch.9) I have suggested that if we want to empower schools and teachers to improve teaching and learning through self-evaluative activity, this has to be supported by values alternative to those which characterise the organisation of many institutions. Current schemes of school self-evaluation are built upon the assumption that they can be accommodated within a structure predicated on existing values. My argument is that if we want schools to engage in evaluation as self-reflexive communities which will take the major responsibility for transformation whether through generating their own reforms or implementing external reforms with a degree of imagination and creativity, this has to be based upon a change in the value structure of schools. Working relationships have to be deduced from autonomy-based accountability rather than power-based responsibility. These values - the exposure of individual work to collective critique within a framework of professional equality requires the setting up of institutional processes which encourage their development. Within this framework it is possible for the school to handle collectively most of the changes demanded of them, whether these are for the appraisal of teachers or of pupils, of the curriculum or of the school as a whole.

The second observation relates to methodology. There are two points here I wish to make. The first concerns techniques or methods. While teachers engaged in school self-evaluation frequently require assistance with refining techniques and more practice at conducting and reporting evaluations, technical skill is not the main issue nor the main preoccupation. Evaluation is establishing the worth of something. Who does that on what criteria and who gets to know about it are the questions that frequently override concerns with improving techniques *per se*. In the past ten years I have conducted numerous in-service courses, which, initially, in response to requests from schools or local authorities have focused upon how to do evaluations, by which is usually meant techniques. (These, of course, are not divorced from assumptions and values about the transmission and utilization of knowledge.) Invariably, especially as individuals and individual schools come to see themselves as the focus of evaluation, attention shifts to a concern with the *data itself* - what kind of data is relevant and in what form - and *procedures for handing that data* - who gets to see it and for what purpose. Once schools have conducted an evaluation or two, these issues come even more to the fore. That evaluation is a political process becomes a reality, both in relation to accountability to one's own colleagues and pupils (often more threatening than to outsiders) and in relation to accountability to outside audiences - parents, the LEA and the wider community. It is at this point, ie once an awareness of the inherent nature of evaluation is experienced, that the utility of establishing ethical procedures for the generation and flow of information is recognised. It is at this point too, (and this is connected with the methodological importance of generating procedures for conducting and reporting evaluations) that schools and individuals come to see the importance of their own agency in the political process. Given appropriate safeguards over the use of information and the organisational framework suggested earlier, they begin to see that they have a positive role to play through an evaluation process in bringing about change in themselves, in their schools, and for their pupils.

This is the major point about the politics of methodology that I want to make. Whether one chooses to observe, interview, analyse documents, generate a questionnaire, analyse examination results or curriculum content or pedagogies; whether one chooses to report the evaluation in a series of classroom observations, issue-focused accounts, a two page executive summary, a statistical analysis or patterns of results, a map of where and how a school stands on a particular issue, through pupil interview transcripts, through a multi-perspective account of an issue or a case study utilizing a narrative form, a dramatic form or an executive form of reporting; whether the evaluation report is more formative or summative in intent, ie raising a series of questions or a future agenda for discussion; all these decisions depend upon prior decisions that need to be taken about who the evaluation is for, why it is being undertaken, what kind of data are needed for this purpose, how it is best communicated and who gets to see the results. The variety of school self-evaluations that can be conducted is quite extensive. Choice of method is directly related to the purpose of the evaluation and the audience for the evaluation.

The second point relates more directly to the process itself. Many of the first wave of school self-evaluation efforts have been characterised by a singular lack of attention to two other essential features of evaluation, criteria for establishing value, and the provision of evidence.

Many of the schemes invite review and judgment certainly (and in any judgment there is likely to be an implicit criterion), but few require that the criteria for these judgments be explicit and that evidence be provided which indicates that the criteria have or have not been met. For school self-evaluation, or any evaluation, to have credibility and development potential, its procedures and process must be open to public scrutiny. Opinion, assertion, unsubstantiated judgment are insufficient grounds for accepting the validity of the evaluation. It is part of the professional role of evaluation to provide a more informed basis for people to make judgments of value. People need to know on what evidence that information is based and in relation to what criteria. This is an essential part of the professionalism I outlined earlier and an essential element in the theory of school development which underpins this process of school self-evaluation. Colleagues, pupils, parents, governors, should be able to participate in the process of evaluation and ideally, in the setting of criteria by which the school determines its worth. This process of establishing criteria and providing an evidential basis for judgment is one which requires further development in school self-evaluation.

This brings me to my third observation about what we have learnt from the second wave of school self-evaluation efforts, and it is that a great deal of back-up support and training is required to establish and maintain school self-evaluation as a process. This observation bears close resemblance to the analysis of many a curriculum reform effort that much support was required to sustain implementation. But the training requirements for evaluation go beyond traditional forms of support and even the acquisition of more highly specific research skills, to training in the art of conducting and disseminating evaluations. There are specific research skills to be acquired, that is true. It is not simply a question of transfer of 'natural practice', though there is a lot that can be built upon. There are fundamental political and ethical questions to confront. There are organisational questions to address. There are political skills to acquire; interpersonal skills to develop and skills of analysing and reporting to improve. Experience of conducting institutional self-evaluation courses indicates quite strongly (from the evidence of the participants themselves) that schools require training in evaluation on these dimensions in addition to the normal innovative support requirements of time, resources and total school and LEA commitment to the task.

If I have made the task of school self-evaluation complex I do not apologise. Change is a difficult process. School self-evaluation that incorporates a model for school development that is educational for all concerned will require a lot of effort, organisation, training and support. But what is encouraging to note after a decade of work in this area is that there is now a greater urgency on the part of schools to engage in institutional development. This has been stimulated perhaps by the demands of GCSE, TVEI, TRIST and GRIST[13] which in many schools and localities has led to collaborative development, but also by the recognition of what schools have already learnt about the process of school evaluation.

SUMMARY AND CONCLUSION

I want to conclude with a future scenario. It was through evaluating the curriculum reform efforts of the late sixties and early seventies that we began to generate a theory of school-based development for change. It was through participation in and evaluation of a new wave of school self-evaluation reform that we are now more informed about what support schools actually need in order to become more effective agents of reform. I have argued that the most promising way forward for reform of schools is through a process of school self-evaluation in which teachers and pupils are at the centre of the evaluation process supporting professional responsibility and accountability for the improvement of their schools. This is not, I have stressed, an insular process solely internal to the school, but rather a first step towards developing the skills and the confidence required to become more professionally accountable. Such a process, I have argued, requires support and training in a number of dimensions.

There are three further steps that need to be taken, steps that I have alluded to earlier in indicating what we have learned, first from the curriculum reform movement, and secondly, from the school self-evaluation movement.

The first lies in an extension of the process of transforming the culture of the school to building a professional culture between schools. This could be accomplished by encouraging pairs of schools, groups of schools and even groups of teachers across schools (though in this case there has to be an equally strong intra-school development focus) to engage in self-evaluation of particular topics and issues of common curriculum concern. Through this process, it is possible to extend the concept of justifiable self-direction, which I see as the essence of an educative approach to evaluation, to generate a culture of inter- professional development.[14]

The second is to build closer links between the local education authority and the schools, for the local education authority to take the initiative in creating the conditions, the structures and the in-service provision necessary to assist schools to develop *as* institutions and *between* institutions. To some extent this is beginning to happen through the new in-service arrangements which are encouraging the generation of institutional development plans and consortia of schools planning their own in-service needs.

The third, and perhaps most crucial, is to extend the boundaries of the school to include parents, governors, employers; and to extend the culture of participation, of self-evaluation and hence of the ownership of any change effort emanating from evaluation to the broader community. This is a complex concept and one not easily accomplished, but some local authorities are making progress in this direction. (see note 14). It requires time to develop the mutual respect and accountability needed to share judgments safely with others. It has to be supported by structures which encourage dialogue, commitment and responsibility for development. It seems facile to say perhaps that what is needed is a greater dialogue between parents, teachers, employers, politicians, governors, schools and academics - all who have an interest at the local level in improving schools. Yet this is what has been missing from two waves of school reform efforts. Many of the centrally developed reforms by-passed the local region; many of the more recent school self-evaluation efforts remained disconnected from their communities.

The school in this scenario is still the basic *unit* of change; teachers the *prime agents* of change.

It is as well to remember, too, that many of the significant educational advances have been achieved in practice, if not initiated by practitioners, even if taken up and reconceptualised later by academics (see Elliott, 1988 for an interesting analysis of the essential origin in practice of many significant educational ideas; see also Whitehead, 1932). The detailed working out of educational ideas takes place in the classroom and by schools themselves. It may well be an interactive process between ideas from central and local authorities, teachers, academics and others (which is where self-evaluation collectively by the school and community has a central role) but it is the schools that interpret and ultimately create the educational experience which flows from them. We would do well to strengthen our schools as the major unit of change by providing the support they require to become better self-evaluative communities and by ensuring that the evaluation processes we ask of them are consistent with these educational aims.

NOTES

1 Murray, F. B. (1986) Goals for the Reform of Teacher Education: an executive summary of the Holmes Group report, Phi Delta Kappa.

2 For further elaboration of this shift in emphasis see Simons, H. (1987) *Getting to Know Schools in a Democracy: the politics and process of evaluation.* Lewes: Falmer Press, ch.1; and Cronbach, L. J. and Associates (1980) *Toward Reform of Program Evaluation: Aims, Methods and Institutional Arrangements.* San Francisco, CA: Jossey Bass.

3 For further descriptions of the canons underlying this approach, see Simons, (1987) op. cit., Guba, E. G. and Lincoln, Y. S. (1981) *Effective Evaluation.* San Francisco, CA: Jossey Bass; and Lincoln, Y. S., and Guba, E. G. (1985) Naturalistic Inquiry. San Francisco, CA: Jossey Bass.

4   The concept of democratic evaluation has as its central aspiration how to find an appropriate balance between the public's right to know and the individual's right to privacy in the conduct and dissemination of evaluation. The concept derives from the rhetoric of liberal democracy, a rhetoric that is morally and politically acceptable to those exercising delegated power. From this rhetoric is derived a set of power equalising procedures that cut into the customary relationships embedded in organisations, holding participants at all levels accountable to criteria endorsed by them. Central precepts in the procedures include confidentiality, negotiation and accessibility. Such procedures cannot, of course, change the power relationships but what they can do is to accord equal treatment to individuals and ideas, establish a flow of information that is independent of hierarchical or powerful interests; and ensure that no one group or person has the power of veto. In such a context all relevant perspectives can be represented, information fairly and equitably exchanged and deliberation encouraged.

   Though frequently interpreted in terms of its applicability to school level evaluation, the concept is equally applicable to all levels of the education system. For further elaboration of the democratic approach to evaluation see MacDonald (1974), MacDonald and Norris (1981) and Simons (1987) (op cit).

5   The 'evaluator as educator' is a term introduced by Cronbach and associates (1980) (op cit) to suggest that instead of aspiring to influence specific decisions, evaluation should adopt a more gradual role of contributing to dialogue and shaping understanding of social programmes and policies, but it is also implicit in the democratic approach to evaluation proposed by MacDonald (1974) in Evaluation and the Control of Education in MacDonald, B. and Walker, R. (1974), *Innovation, Evaluation, Research and the Problem of Control.* Norwich: Centre for Applied Research in Education; and the concept of responsive evaluation proposed by Stake, R. E. (ed) (1975) *Evaluating the Arts in Education; a responsive approach.* Columbus, Ohio: Charles Merrill Publishing Company, both of which aspire to educate the judgments of a variety of consumers of education.

6   For further discussion of the teacher-as-researcher concept, see Stenhouse, L. (1975) *An Introduction to Curriculum Research and Development*, London: Heinemann; and Elliott, J. (1976) 'Developing hypotheses from teachers' practical constructs', *Interchange*, 7(2), 2-22.

7   For further comment on the school self-evaluation movement, its origins, purposes and forms see Simons (1987) (op cit) and Clift et al (1987) *Studies in School Self-Evaluation*. Lewes: Falmer Press.

8   For further elaboration of this approach, see Simons, H. (1981) Process evaluation in schools, in Lacey, C. and Lawton, D. (eds) *Issues in Accountability and Evaluation*. London: Methuen, 114-44.

9   For an outline of the GRIDS project see McMahon, A., Bolam, R., Abbott, R. and Holly, P. (1984) *Guidelines for Review and Internal Development in Schools: secondary schools handbook*, Schools Council Publications, York: Longman; and for comment upon it see Holly, P. (1984) The institutionalisation of action-research in schools, *Cambridge Journal of Education*, 14, 2, 5-18; Simons (1987) (op cit) ch.9; and Hopkins, D.

10 For a critique of LEA-initiated school self-evaluation schemes, see Clift et al (1987) (op cit) Simons (1987) (op cit ch.9) and Simons (1986)

11 In 1986, the scheme for funding in-service education in the UK changed from one that allowed local education authorities primarily to establish their own priorities for in-service training and to second individual teachers to full-time one year masters' courses to one that involved local education authorities in making a bid for central government funds, sixty per cent of which have to be in relation to national priorities, forty per cent local priorities. It is within this broad framework that some LEAs are involving their schools in developing institutional development plans as a first step in establishing their local bid.

12 With the advent of the 1988 Education Act, financial management is being devolved locally to schools according to formulae determined by each local education authority.

13 GCSE (General Certificate of Secondary Education)
TVEI (Technical and Vocational Education Initiative)
TRIST (TVEI-related In-Service Training)
GRIST (Grant-related In-service Training)

14 See Simons, H, Elliott, J and MacDonald, B (1987) *Kettering Alternative Approach: independent external evaluation report on the second year, 1986-7*, for one example of how six schools have collaborated to improve learning opportunities and the curriculum across the town.

References
CLIFT, P. S., NUTTALL, D. L.*and* McCORMICK, R. (eds) (1987) *Studies in School Self-Evaluation.* Lewes: Falmer Press.

ELLIOTT, J. (1988) The Teacher as Researcher: implications for the supervision of teachers. Invited address to the American Educational Research Association's Annual Meeting, New Orleans.

HOUSE, E. R. (1980) Technology versus Craft: a ten year perspective on innovation. In: TAYLOR, P. H. (1979) *New Directions in Curriculum Studies.* Lewes: Falmer Press

HOUSE, E. R. *and* LAPAN, S. (1988) Teacher Appraisal. In: SIMONS, H. and ELLIOTT, J. (eds) (1989) *Rethinking Assessment and Appraisal.* Milton Keynes: Open University Press.

HOYLE, E. W. (1975) The creativity of the school in Britain. In : HARRIS, A., LAWN, M. and PRESCOTT, W. (eds) *Curriculum Innovation.* London: Croom Helm in association with the Open University Press.

MacDONALD, B. (1974) Evaluation and the Control of Education. In: MacDONALD, B. and WALKER, R. (eds) *Innovation, Evaluation, Research and the Problem of Control.* Norwich: Centre for Applied Research in Education.

MacDONALD, B. (1981) Interviewing in case study evaluation, Phi Delta Kappa, *CEDR Quarterly,* 14, Bloomington, Ind.

MacDONALD, B. *and* NORRIS, N. (1981) Looking up for a change - political horizons in policy evaluation, Norwich, Centre for Applied Research in Education, University of East Anglia, mimeo. An earlier version of this paper is published in POPKEWITZ, T. S. and TABACHNIK, B. R. (1981) *The Study of Schooling: field based methodologies in educational research and evaluation.* New York: Praeger.

MURRAY, F. B. (1986) Goals for the Reform of Teacher Education: an executive summary of the Holmes Group report, Phi Delta Kappa.

NATIONAL COMMISSION ON EXCELLENCE IN EDUCATION (1983) *A Nation at Risk: the imperative for educational reform.* Washington, DC: US Department of Education.

PATTON, M. Q. (1978) *Utilization-Focused Evaluation.* Beverly Hills, CA: Sage Publications.

REID, W. A. (1987) Institutions and Practices: professional education reports and the language of reform, *Educational Researcher*, November, 10-15

SCRIVEN, M. (1967) The methodology of evaluation. In: TYLER, R. W., GAGNE, R. M. and SCRIVEN, M. (1967) *Perspectives of Curriculum Evaluation.* American Educational Research Association Monograph Series on Curriculum Evaluation, 1. Chicago: Rand McNally.

SHIPMAN, M. (1983) Styles of school-based evaluations. In: GALTON, M. and MOON, B. (eds) *Changing Schools ... Changing Curriculum:* 248-54. London: Harper and Row.

SIMONS, H. *(1981)* 'Process evaluation in schools. In: LACEY, C. and LAWTON, D. (eds) Issues in Accountability and Evaluation. 114-44. London: Methuen.

SIMONS, H. (1986) School Self-evaluation: a critique of Local Education Authority initiated schemes, paper presented at AERA, the American Educational Research Association's Annual Meeting, San Francisco.

SIMONS, H. (1987) *Getting to Know Schools in a Democracy: the politics and process of evaluation.* Lewes: Falmer Press.

SIZER, T. (1988) In: TIMAR, T. B. and KIRP, D. (1988) *Managing Educational Excellence*, p xi. Lewes: Falmer Press.

SMITH, L. M., KLEINE, P. F., PRUNTY, J. P. and DWYER, D. C. (1987) *Educational Innovators: then and now.* Book I of the Trilogy *Anatomy of Educational Innovation: a mid to long term re-study and reconstrual.* Lewes: Falmer Press.

TIMAR, T. B. *and* KIRP, D. L. (1988) *Managing Educational Excellence.* Lewes: Falmer Press.

WHITEHEAD, A. N. (1932) *The Aims of Education and Other Essays.* London: Ernest Benn.

WISE, A. E., DARLING-HAMMOND, L., McLAUGHLIN, M. *and* BERNSTEIN, H., (1984) *Teacher Evaluation: a study of effective practices.* The Rand Corporation for the National Institute of Education.

4
A Structure for Evaluation to Meet the Needs of a Decentralised Reform Strategy in Upper Secondary Education in Sweden

Lars Johansson
Swedish National Board of Education, Stockholm

SUMMARY

In 1984 the Riksdag (ie the Swedish parliament) passed a Bill, introduced by the Social Democratic Government, for the inauguration of a scheme of experimentation and development in upper secondary schools.

One of the basic ideas of the Government Bill, entitled Upper Secondary Schools in Transition, was for development work to be conducted on a sound local footing and for local initiatives and experience to be utilized during the five-year period for which the project was to last.

At the same time the National Board of Education was given the task of drawing up a programme of experimentation and development, defining models and guidelines for the project. That programme indicated the main outlines of the evaluative work which was to be planned and conducted parallel to the development work. The evaluation is to form the basis of future reform decisions, in addition to supporting and encouraging the development work as such. An evaluative organisation has been built up at local school level, within the county education committees and between them, within the higher education regions and at the National Board of Education.

In addition to the evaluation which is being undertaken at individual upper secondary schools and within the administration, parts of the national assignment are being performed by independent evaluators at a number of educational and other departments of universities and university colleges.

The evaluation is to be conducted between 1985 and 1990. It has been allotted an annual State budget of about MSEK 12 in the form of earmarked funds.

The activities are resulting among other things in a large number of annual reports, of which the national report to the Government is being printed in book form and distributed in large numbers to upper secondary schools and educational interests.

HOW WE DO EVALUATIONS
Experimentation and Development in Upper Secondary Schools

On 7th June 1984 the Riksdag resolved on the inauguration of a process of experimentation and development in upper secondary schools. The Social Democratic Government had introduced proposals to this effect in the Riksdag, in a Bill entitled 'Upper Secondary Schools in Transition' (1983/84: 116).

In this Bill, it was proposed that:
a successive reform be implemented, starting with a wide-ranging scheme of experimentation and development;
the work of reform be conducted in close co-operation with active members of the upper secondary school community - teachers, students and school management - so that local experience and initiative could be utilized in the ongoing process of renewal;
the process of experimentation and development be concentrated mainly within a five-year period, starting in 1984/85. Experiments beginning in 1985/86 are also to continue for five years. It is anticipated that certain proposals can be implemented earlier, once 'development work has yielded documentation on which to base the more detailed regulation of the activities', as the Government Bill puts it.

The Bill also emphasises that the experimentation and development proposed affect all decision-making levels in school. Reference is made to the 'great importance of teachers, students and school managements, municipal and regional educational authorities and the whole of the national school administration playing an active part in the activities and having an opportunity of sharing in responsibility for it and control of it'.

Local Decision-making Responsibility and Central Management by Objectives

At a symposium in Uppsala in March 1985, entitled 'Upper secondary schools in transition - reform strategies and evaluative models', the Minister of Education, Lena Hjelm Wallén, expounded her views, and those of the Government, on the experimentation and development which had then been in progress for one year:

> One relevant question, of course, is whether a process of experimentation and development can yield tenable solutions for achieving the goals I have outlined in the Government Bill entitled Upper Secondary Schools in Transition. In my opinion, the basic prerequisites for achieving the goals do already exist.
>
> *One* such prerequisite is that of general and widespread support for the general objectives laid down for the development of upper secondary schools, Support of this kind exists not only in the Riksdag but also in extensive circles among those who are active in schools and elsewhere within the education system.
>
> A *second* prerequisite is for activities to be conducted in close collaboration with the people affected by them in schools. This has been guaranteed through the strategy adopted for renewal and for the implementation of the new ideas.
>
> A *third* prerequisite is for activities to be planned in such a way that they can and will be evaluated. Evaluation, as I see it, is important in several different ways. The individual school must get into the habit of defining goals for its activities and then successively making sure that its own activities are evaluated. Local evaluation and information dissemination to people who are locally active, concerning the progress of particular experiments, is thus a supremely essential task of evaluation.
>
> At central level, evaluation is required to yield serviceable input documentation on which to base future reforming decisions. Answers are needed, for example, to questions relating to the possibility of generalising experiments and making them a foundation of general changes, as well as questions relating to financial consequences.

The Minister's view of evaluation is both interesting and thought-provoking. Evaluation, thus seen, is not only the consequence of a reforming decision but also an integral part of a development strategy - 'One prerequisite is for activities to be planned in such a way that they can and will be evaluated.'

Evaluation must make it possible to follow and verify efforts to realise the centrally-defined objectives. But evaluation is also attributed with an essential role within the individual school. Now that the details of school work are no longer governed by regulations and allocations, each school has to shape its own activities within the allotted scope. This implies a responsibility for following and evaluating effects and results and for distributing information about them. In this way, local evaluation takes on a supportive role in relation to development. Thus we find evaluation, during a phase of reform which, in addition to specific curricular renewal, is generally characterised by decentralisation, acquiring a variety of tasks, depending on the level at which it takes place.

The Government's 1987 Budget Bill makes it clear that the view concerning the terms of development expressed in the Government's Bill 'Upper Secondary Schools in Transition' in 1984 has, if anything, acquired greater emphasis during the intervening years. The following statement of principle comes from the Minister of Education, Bengt Göransson:

> The most important resource in schools, apart from the pupils themselves, is the teachers and other staff working there. Their commitment is essential in order for schools to succeed in their difficult and important task of transmitting knowledge and skills to the pupils and developing the pupils' personalities.
>
> This makes it necessary for the changes which we wish to introduceas a means of improving schools to be found justifiable by the persons who have to put them into effect. You cannot transform schools without the support of the people who work in them. Schools can only be developed with their staff. Another essential prerequisite is for the community at large to help draw attention to the position of teachers, as a foundation for development work undertaken in the school sector.

Thus far the Swedish Minister of Education, Bengt Göransson. The development of local decision-making responsibilities, in other words, is a salient principle in the renewal of youth education. The fundamental motive is confidence in teachers' professional acumen and in school organisation. It is, however, important to note that this principle does not imply any relaxation of aims where national political control is concerned. If anything, ongoing decentralisation accentuates the need for national formulation of objectives and management by objectives, ie the definition of goals as frames or guidelines which - within the fields where the State reserves its prerogative

- define the scope for local liberty. This makes evaluation the prime instrument for following, scrutinising and appraising the realisation of educational objectives.

The Main Outlines of the Government Bill 'Upper Secondary Schools in Transition'

The aims of the experimentation and development proposed in the Bill can be summarised under five heads:

1. An upper secondary school which is accessible and meaningful to all young persons.

2. Greater organisational and structural flexibility in order to cater to the needs of the labour market and to individual preferences.

3. Development of the internal work of upper secondary schools, so as to improve the prospects of teachers and students adapting teaching to local needs, adopting delegated decision-making responsibilities and a democratic working organisation.

4. Wider co-operation between education and working life and integration of theory and practice.

5. Co-operation between upper secondary schools and adult education, so as to develop opportunities of recurrent education with due respect and consideration for the education needs of different groups.

On each of the points, the Government Bill includes concrete proposals concerning development inputs.

Planning Work Within the National School Administration, 1983/84

Sweden's national school administration consists of the National Board of Education (NBE) and of 24 county education committees - one per county. The present organisation and structure of responsibilities within the administration, dating from 1982, imply, briefly, that the NBE is responsible for national planning, curricular development and evaluation while the county education committees have a number of operational planning and supervisory duties and are responsible for direct contacts with schools and local education authorities.

During the spring of 1983 it became clear to the senior officials of the NBE and the county education committees that the process of reform in upper secondary schools, which had been under investigation since 1976. would have to begin with an extensive process of experimentation and development, based on and partly initiated through decisions by schools and municipalities.

How was this reforming strategy to be handled within the national school administration? The task of developing and administering the process of experimentation and development would not necessarily be entrusted to the NBE and the county education committees at all. The Swedish Trade Union Confederation (LO) had proposed the appointment of a parliamentary education commission, a proposal which also had other advocates.

On the other hand, the strategy adopted was a test for the new organisation acquired by the national school administration as a result of the 1982 Riksdag Resolution. The re-organisation had stressed the responsibility of the NBE for long-term school development, planning and evaluation, at the same time as responsibility for field contacts and for the supervision of development work in schools was transferred to the county education committees. This apportionment role between the NBE and the county education committees dovetailed neatly with the reform strategy adopted, which called for an efficient 'locomotive' in every county. The intention was for the county education committees to discharge this function.

The first measure taken was an invitation to all local education authorities in municipalities with upper secondary schooling to state their interest in taking part in a process of experimentation and development.

There were several reasons why it was found essential for work to begin with an invitation of this kind. For one thing it underlined the reforming strategy advocated, and then again it could lead to the inauguration of development work in schools and municipalities. Thus there was a mobilisation aspect present in the deliberations prompting the invitation. Another reason was that the answers received ought reasonably to enable us to assess the interest aroused by development work and the course it was likely to take.

The NBE's invitation to the local education authorities met with a surprisingly powerful response. More than 1,600 expressions of interest were received by the county education committees, and about 850 of them were judged relevant to the reforming process. The others were of more specifically local interest or else fell outside the frames defined for the evaluation of suggestions.

Those who had believed upper secondary schools to be generally uninterested in development work and change now had cause for reflection. At the same time, of course, there was discussion of the practical conditions and prospects for individual schools and municipalities influencing future reforming decisions. Would it be possible to combine central political visions and initiatives with local ideas and preferences? Would not the latter invariably have to defer to the former?

The answer to that question hinges, logically, on the extent of the frames which the central political and administrative system is prepared to concede for local liberty and implementation and on whether the content of those frames would be found relevant and meaningful by the people employed in schools.

In this respect, our hopes in 1983 concerning general authorisation from the Government were not borne out by events. There are several reasons for this. With local implementation of the study organisation, it proved difficult to restrain the growth of expenditure. Unwillingness to accept the full consequences of delegating decisions and decentralising activities could be another reason.

The comprehensive material emerging from the notifications of interest given by the municipalities was classified, registered and computer-processed at the NBE, to provide the foundation of work on a programme of experimentation and a development which was to present models and suggestions for development work. At the same time a procedure for consultation was opened up with representative organisations of teachers and school management. Representatives of the different trade union organisations played an active part in the drafting work of various study groups.

One vital question which arose at an early stage concerned the extent to which efforts should be made to achieve a consensus with the trade union organisations. We took the view that, without such a consensus, experimentation and development in individual schools would be greatly impeded. This, however, was not merely acceptance of a negotiating situation whose basic conditions were dictated by the strategy adopted. It is a view based on the conviction that genuine development work calls for personal involvement and professional interest on the part of teachers and school managements. Far too many reforms in the school sector in Sweden have stopped short at theoretical constructions in Government Bills, Riksdag Resolutions, curricula etc. We now want to conduct a full-scale experiment, making use of the entire administration at central, regional and local levels, so as to establish favourable conditions for local development work in line with central policy objectives. One necessary, although insufficient ingredient, in this case, was consensus between the parties most immediately affected.

In March 1984 the Government introduced its Bill 'Upper Secondary Schools in Transition', which made it possible for subsequent drafting work to be conducted on a firmer, although narrower basis.

Up until the Riksdag Resolution in June, our programming work was entirely of a preparatory nature. Following the Riksdag Resolution of 7th

June, the NBE was formerly commissioned by the Government to draw up a programme of experimentation and development in upper secondary schools. The remit was to be completed not later than 30th June 1984. The NBE Directorate finalised the programme at the end of the month. Work had then been in progress, parallel to the drafting of the Government Bill in the Government Chancery, since the spring of 1983. The programme also deals with the evaluation which was to proceed parallel to the development process. The purposes and structure of the evaluation were made clear.

General Description of the Evaluative Assignment
The background to the current evaluation of experimentation and development work in upper secondary schools has been sketched in sections 1-4, so that readers unfamiliar with school developments in Sweden will be able to follow and appraise the ensuing account of the evaluation process, in particular the structural aspects.

This section describes the purpose and design of the evaluation as decided by the NBE in June 1984. The sections which follow give a fairly detailed account of the different parts of the evaluative structure as implemented between 1985/86 and 1987/88.

In the Riksdag debate on the Upper Secondary Schools Bill, particular emphasis was laid on development questions. The Liberal and Moderate Parties above all emphasised the need for an objective and credible evaluation. It soon became clear to the NBE that the impending period of experimentation and development would require evaluation measures of a very special order. An evaluative organisation would have to be built up, specially geared to the reforming strategy. The coming situation would be characterised by a diversity of projects and participating schools. Projects would be starting at different times in different schools. The schools taking part would also have varying numbers of projects of various degrees of complexity. And each school would have to be treated as a unique environment in a number of vital respects.

The evaluation would have to measure up to high standards of objectivity and credibility. There were, of course, practical reasons for this, but the same considerations were heightened by the political sensitivity of the question as revealed by the Riksdag debate. Apart from these requirements, the evaluation would have to encourage and support development work by means of vigorous, continuous feedback of results to the people taking part in projects in the individual schools.

Purposes of the evaluation as defined in the NBE's programme of experimentation and development.
The programme of experimentation and development defines two main purposes for the evaluation:
1. The evaluation results are an important basis for decisions by the Government and Riksdag concerning further activities. This calls for a high standard of security and dependability in the evaluation.
2. The evaluation must encourage commitment and "developmentality" at all levels of the school system. The supportive, stimulatory function is addressed above all to schools taking part in experimentation and development work. The evaluation will provide an important foundation for that work through the feedback of results to teachers and to those in charge of local experiments.

Scheme of evaluation
The aims of the evaluation naturally have an impact on organisational and methodological aspects. The results of the experimentation and development work are to be codified and appraised in a national perspective, as a foundation for future reforming decisions. This has been provided for through the creation of national evaluative resources. Extensive self-contained evaluation assignments have been distributed by the NBE, mainly to education departments of universities and university colleges. This has been done in two ways, viz more traditionally defined thematic evaluative assignments, in which a particular question is evaluated with reference to predefined criteria, and secondly in the form of 'case studies', in which the school as a whole constitutes the evaluative target and the environment and conditions in the local community governing the working conditions of the school can be taken into account in the evaluation.

The separate research-based evaluation is being supplemented by extensive activities conducted in schools and within the national school administration.

Evaluation at school level has the important task of encouraging those taking part in the development work to reflect on and analyse their own activities. Evaluation at local level, however, has also been allotted a role in the national programme. To facilitate the evaluative work of the county education committees, co-operation was established between them in the country's five higher education regions. To this end, special regional co-ordinating officers were appointed prior to the 1985/86 school year.

In the concluding phase of evaluation, the NBE describes and evaluates experimentation and development work on the basis of reports supplied by the independent researchers and also with reference to reports produced within the administration. The NBE presents its assessments to the Government in an annual report. So far, reports of this kind have been presented for the 1985/86 and 1986/87 school years. The report for 1987/88 is now in preparation, for presentation during the autumn of 1988.

Different Levels of Evaluation

At local level, evaluation is being conducted by the schools concerned. Roughly 300 out of Sweden's more than 500 upper secondary schools are involved. At county level, this work is the responsibility of the county education committee, which presents an annual report to the NBE, giving a concise picture and assessment of the state of experimentation and development work in its county. The regional co-ordinating officers, who are responsible primarily for the co-ordination of evaluative work between the county education committees in each higher education region, present an annual thematic report to the NBE. The work done at the various levels will be briefly described in this section.

Local levels

The main purpose of local evaluation is to record activities and, through local reports, to supply local (municipal) education authorities and, above all, county education committees, with input documentation. Otherwise local evaluation can meet the requirements defined by the individual school. To perform these tasks, local evaluators are appointed at the schools concerned. The evaluator is most often a teacher, sometimes a headteacher, whose teaching duties are reduced accordingly. In other words, the State pays for these duties to be performed. The reduction of teaching duties can vary, but on average it is three periods per week. Total State expenditure on local evaluators amounts to some MSEK 7.5.

The regional co-ordinating officers inaugurated a comprehensive scheme of basic evaluation methods training for local evaluators. Based on the higher education regions and in collaboration with the higher education INSET organisation, a large number of courses have been completed, usually with a total time input of 5 weeks. This has appreciably elevated the general level of knowledge and evaluation methods in Swedish upper secondary schools and, of course, has made the people concerned better equipped for the task of evaluation.

County level

The county education committees are required to maintain specialist competence in the field of evaluation, and nowadays they invariably do so. At the beginning of the period there were considerable shortfalls in competence which the evaluative assignment made it possible to work off. It is important for evaluative competence to be combined with a thorough knowledge of upper secondary school and/or adult education and its developmental issues.

The evaluation undertaken by the county education committees is required to supply the State with the input information it requires for decision-making and also to shed light on ways in which regional interests can be turned to account in the development of upper secondary schooling.

The work of the county education committees must have both a supportive and a reporting function. Schools and municipalities need help with INSET, goal formulation and planning.

The regional co-ordinating officers responsible for co-ordinating evaluative activities in the broad sense within a higher education region also submit an annual report to the NBE. Unlike the county education committees, which are required to supply a comprehensive picture of work in their several counties, the co-ordinating officers have to undertake an in-depth analysis of a particular field. Their analytical themes are chosen in consultation with evaluation officers at the NBE, with whom the regional co-ordinating officers co-operate very closely. There are at present five regional co-ordinating officer appointments. Since 1985/86 these have been held by elderly, highly qualified and scientifically eminent educationalists, which has meant a great deal, not least to the initiating of INSET and development within schools and administrations.

Central level
The main duty of the NBE, on the basis of descriptions contained by local evaluative reports, research-based evaluation, situation reports, information from the county education committees and statistical material, is to evaluate the extent, structure and outcome of the experimentation and development work in progress. This evaluation is to provide the basis for decisions by NBE about new experimental activities and for policy decisions by the Government and Riksdag.

The department responsible for upper secondary schools includes a special evaluative unit with a staff of about 10. One of the main tasks of this group is to take charge of the administration and direction of the evaluative assignment described here.

The annual report submitted to the Government by the NBE is drafted by a number of groups in which the units of the NBE responsible for different subjects and syllabi are represented. The drafting stage also has input from representatives of the county education committees and the regional co-ordinating officers. Special scrutinies and analyses are entrusted to appropriately qualified researchers. For this central, national part of the evaluative assignment, the NBE has at its disposal an annual budget of some MSEK 5. Most of this budget goes on the independent, research-based part of the evaluation.

As has been made clear, the evaluation, inevitably, is dependent on a large number of reports. The large volume of written documentation involves problems with which the majority of people who have been involved in major evaluative projects are likely to be familiar. The structure of the reports will be described in somewhat greater detail in a concluding section. First, however, I propose dealing with two more sources on the evaluative work of the NBE, viz base information and research-based case studies.

Base Information
The evaluative process involves dealing with more than 1,000 separate development projects. Each project is identified by a project number, comprising the county initial and a serial number. (Every county in Sweden is represented by one or two letters of the alphabet.) This identification accompanies the project whenever it is referred to (in local reports, county reports, etc). "Base information" comprises quantitative data about the projects, furnishing input material for a database at the NBE.

Every year the schools taking part supply certain particulars about development projects, eg study programmes affected, numbers of students and staff affected, funding etc. These base information forms (two in number) are transmitted to the appropriate county education committee, for checking. Some counties transmit their base information to the NBE by diskette or data communication, and the aim is for all county education committees to do so. The base information supplies the NBE with an up-to-date database on development work in upper secondary schools, thus providing quantitative overviews for evaluative purposes.

Case Studies
One precondition in designing the evaluative assignment was that a substantial component of the national evaluation was to be undertaken separately from and independent of the administration. It also seemed natural and in keeping with tradition to engage the education departments of universities and university colleges for these assignments. The discussion came to centre round the construction of the assignments, and it continues to do so.

We felt it was reasonable that the research-based evaluation should also be brought into line with the reforming strategy and that special attention should thus be paid to the local conditions which, we assumed, would vary from one school to another ('grammar schools' - 'trade schools'), or from one environment to another (eg countryside and big city), and which we expected would influence the scope and direction of development work. We considered it vital for this totality to be subjected to evaluation , and we therefore advocated a case study approach on these terms.

The traditional research-based evaluation applied usually employed a thematic, highly rational approach. A change in the situation at a particular level is evaluated with reference to an array of pre-defined criteria. The criteria are defined with reference to the centrally-specified goals of the change and in keeping with a uniform national frame of reference.

About twenty schools in Sweden with a notable range of experimental activities were designated case study schools and about ten case study evaluators were contracted by the NBE to observe development work at these schools for the period ending 1988/89. The case study evaluators have formalised contacts between them through a consulting forum headed by Professor Ulf P Lundgren, who has an outstanding international reputation and is active at the Stockholm Institute of Education and elsewhere. The evaluators are required to report to the NBE. The structure and methodology of the case studies and the presentation of findings are decided quite independently by the client, the NBE, and are not subject to any partite influence.

This work has been described in annual reports, which constitute a vital foundation of NBE assessments but have also gained appreciation in the administration at large and on the part of individual schools.

One question of method which has been discussed by the case study evaluators and between them and the administration concerns what may be termed 'thematisation within the framework of the case study'. These matters have been aptly described at the Department of Education, University of Göteborg, by Dr Rolf Lander, the case study evaluator in charge. By reproducing part of a private letter from Dr Lander I would like to illustrate this question, as well as conveying some insight into a case study.

> If case-studies are narrowed down, with schools as cases, this means that the projects have to be considered mainly in a school perspective and in the perspective of a reforming strategy. The input documentation for the NBE centres mainly round the reforming strategy, not so much round the content of the project in itself. This is necessary in terms of sheer resources. Today we have 45 projects at the 6 schools, and at least 13-14 different types of project.

If case studies are narrowed down, taking projects or types of project as cases, one thus achieves what we have now termed thematisation, which calls for a good deal of weeding out among the projects one is interested in and, preferably, a selection of schools based on their relevance to the theme.

Theoretically, a design can be allowed to come anywhere on a sliding scale between schools and projects respectively as the main concern of the case study. In practical terms, the economics of intellectual exertion and work input demand reasonably distinct boundaries.

Thematisation should focus on the projects aiming primarily to achieve (i) a transformation of teacher-pupil relations, including a greater measure of social responsibility for pupils on the part of teachers and (ii) a different view of subject content and working methods of teaching.

These projects challenge the structure and content of relations, the teacher's role and subject teaching. On a general theoretical plane, the challenge can be formulated in Bernstein's paired concepts of classification (surveillance of subject boundaries) and frame (control of the school and teaching process).

There are several projects representing these challenges. And perhaps they imply greater changes in schools which, through their structure of study programmes (lines), most resemble 'the old gymnasium' or 'grammar school' if you so will. Four of the six schools are of this kind.

Concept	Theme	Projects
	Teacher-pupil relations	More active form teachers
		Teacher influence
Framing	Social responsibility for pupils	Study contract
		Subject-related practice
	Working methods	Interdisciplinary approach
		Certain general time schedule subjects
Classification	Subject content	Education for small businesses
		Thematic studies

Projects concerning the transition between upper secondary school and compulsory school can come in the framing category if they deal with the relational side of pupil adjustment to upper secondary school, but hardly if they are information programmes pure and simple.

Thematisation means the NBE getting better input documentation for decisions concerning these particular types of project and their curricular implications, studied in the perspective indicated by our frame of reference.

Other projects thus form the background to our studies. This applies mainly to projects which, above all, are concerned with efficiency improvements in existing subject content and methods, eg different forms of back-up teaching. These are appraised on a more integral basis and also in contrast with the projects more emphatically concerned with change.

We wish to emphasise that no disrespect is intended to projects aimed above all at improving the efficiency of teaching. As teachers ourselves, we are profoundly aware of the need for this. The focus of our interest may give the impression that we have come out in favour of national goals in a reforming strategy which, at the same time, is intended to unite local and central initiatives. We wish to emphasise our intention of subjecting the projects to critical appraisal in a local perspective as well. Since the projects chosen are more demanding and, locally, more controversial, it is not unreasonable that they should be given priority in the evaluation.

Structure of the Report

The following description of purposes and content requirements is intended for those wishing more detailed information on the requirements which have to be met by the different reports.

Local reports

The individual schools supply local reports to the county education committees, supplementing the base information lists. The local reports consist mainly of descriptions from each of the different projects, but they can also be made to include more general information and remarks from those in charge of experimentation at the individual schools.

Purpose: To identify the specific problems and experiences of the local school, together with its recommendations and wishes for the future, against the background of completed/current projects and against the background of school activities generally.

The report supplements and fleshes out the information obtained through the standardised base information lists.

The local report has to contain the best possible descriptions of the individual projects. It is also essential for the persons involved to reflect on their own activities, so as to heighten their insight, knowledge and competence. Local reporting, thus viewed, forms part of an INSET process. Demands concerning the content and design of reports ought therefore to be made more stringent as time goes on.

Content: The county education committees should indicate a structure for the local reports. Certain points should be common to all projects, viz:
1. Concise description of the aims of the project.
2. Anticipated positive effects, in as concrete terms as possible (eg reduced absenteeism, better subject knowledge).
3. Negative effects feared.
4. Structure of the project.
5. Results.
6. Concise verdict.

It is the task of the county education committees to supply schools with more detailed instructions. To support them in this, the regional co-ordinating officers have suggested ways in which the local reports can be structured.

Viewpoints are required from the school management/experimental management in the individual school as to whether the projects inaugurated are those which are most essential from the school's viewpoints. Has the school suggested other projects?

For the first year, the demands made on local reporting should not be too burdensome. Eventually the aim should be to relate the different projects to one another and to other activities of the school concerned. The following questions - not in ranking order, are intended as examples to illustrate this point:

> To what extent is the work of the project based on a genuinely experienced problem? This being so, what is the problem which the project is trying to process and find a better solution to? Better for whom?

Which people/officers have formulated the problem - students, teachers, parents, local school politicians, school management, the teachers' union representatives, other school staff etc.?

Have similar attempts been made previously at the school or at schools known to the staff?

To what extent and in what way is the local (municipal) education authority involved in the activities?

Has the availability of extra funds influenced the inclination to engage in project work? If so, in what ways?

If extra funds are not available, will the school have to revise its priorities? If so, what disadvantages will this entail to other students and other school staff?

Input documentation: Personal observations (in classrooms and during breaks - talking to students and teachers etc), surveys (structured interviews and observations or simple questionnaires, studies of available statistics etc.).

Reports by county education committees
Purpose: To get the county education committee to describe problems and evaluate the development potential of upper secondary schools in the county, as well as to elicit the county education committee's recommendations and wishes for the future.

The county reports should both summarise local reports and include an independent assessment of total experimental activities in the county. Every such report should give as complete a picture as possible of experimentation and development. The reports should mainly include descriptions and assessments of problems and development opportunities in the county's upper secondary schools, as compared with the goals of the development work.

Content:
1. No projects in experimental activities (defined as projects on the official project list).
2. Breakdown by experimental fields, ie classification into main and subsidiary fields, eg concentrated studies, project studies, classroom democracy.

3   How many students are affected by experiments as per point 1? How large a proportion is this of the total student population? And teachers? Breakdown by study programmes, sex, age, etc.
4   Are others besides upper secondary school students involved, eg Komvux (municipal adult education) students or young persons under the mandatory follow-up scheme?
5   How much other experimental activity is there off the central list?
6   Organisation of the experiments. To what extent does a steering group exist for the overall scheme of experimentation?
7   What financial resources have been allotted for the experiments? How much of this money comes from the county education committee development grant, how much is being put up by the municipalities themselves? What about the breakdown between teacher costs and equipment?
8   Outcome of experimental activities in relation to the pre-defined goals. Have the results come up to expectation? Have the anticipated negative effects materialised?
9   General verdict from students, teachers, school management and other staff.
10 Are the activities to be continued/reduced/augmented/discontinued? Any changes?
11 Other points which the county education committees see fit to report concerning the experiments, by way of analysing and appraising the material.

Here are some examples of other questions:

What specific conditions prevail within the county for profiling a certain kind of development work?

Which problems are of such a kind as to require central attention and central inputs?

Description and analysis of the way in which local and county education authorities interpret and implement/realise the central intentions underlying the reforming activities for the development of upper secondary schools.

What support is the committee giving to schools conducting the experimental activities in project form (problem processing, consulting assistance, evaluation, INSET, seminars, etc.)?

What use is the county making of experience from project work in its total work on upper secondary school development in the county?

How does the county education committee view the role of projects in the development of upper secondary schooling in relation to local/ municipal objectives and the local ambitions and circumstances of different schools?

What measures would the county education committee recommend with regard to continuing activities? (Goals, content, framing rules, resources, decision-making procedures etc.)

Several of the above points are of such a kind that the county education committees cannot be expected to be in a position to deal with them when submitting their first report. Here, as in the case of local reports, the principle must be for the depth of reporting to be gradually augmented.

Input documentation: Local reports, visits to schools, statistics, independent surveys, observations and expert inputs; talks with members of local education authorities.

Reports by the regional co-ordinating officers
Purpose: To obtain a descriptive analysis of projects and of regular activities at upper secondary schools in the region.
  Regional reports should not aim at giving a comprehensive picture. (This is done by the county reports.) Instead regional reports deal with interesting regional problems of relevance to current objectives.
  Analysis of conditions, difficulties and impediments within the region as regards the principal aim of achieving an upper secondary school for all youngsters under 20 by making upper secondary schooling more flexible.
  Assessment of INSET needs of upper secondary school staff.

Input documentation: County reports, available statistics, certain local evaluative reports and independent observations. Contacts with case study evaluators and other evaluative researchers in upper secondary schools.

Case study reports
Purpose: On the basis of central guidelines (eg upper secondary schools in transition) and the competence of individual selected researchers, to compile

descriptive analyses of problems and activities at 20 or more selected case study schools.

Separate, independent scientific analysis.

Input documentation: The researcher's own collection of data and other relevant material.

Thematic reports
Purpose: To describe and analyse specific practical issues (eg a new study route) defined by the NBE.

In keeping with the competence of individual selected researchers, to obtain descriptive analyses of problems and activities in relation to specified Riksdag policy decisions.

Separate, independent scientific analysis.

Input documentation: The researcher's own collection of data and other relevent material.

Central reports
Purpose: To compile a concise, descriptive analysis of problems and opportunities in the county's upper secondary schools and to make recommendations to the Government for the future.

Description and analysis of problems and opportunities in Sweden's upper secondary schools, in relation to the operational goals defined by the Government and Riksdag in the Government Bill on Upper Secondary Schools in Transition and in subsequent Riksdag decisions.

This report is submitted annually to the Government, following a timetable laid down for the five-year period which has been fixed, so that the experimental activities will furnish input documentation for policy decisions concerning the ongoing reform of upper secondary schooling.

Input documentation: The relevant documents contained by the above mentioned summary of reports and evaluations, centrally compiled statistical data ('school statistics' from Statistics Sweden etc.), reports on other evaluations and surveys of relevance to the upper secondary school.

So far one central national report has been submitted by the NBE, for the 1985/86 and 1986/87 school years. The 1987/88 report, to be presented in the autumn of 1988, is now being prepared at the NBE.

5
How Are Evaluations Used Today?

A Hussenet
Ministère de l'Education Nationale, Paris

OUTLINE
Introduction
Preliminary Remarks
 1 Definition
 2 Giving evaluation its proper place and value
 3 Use of evaluations: a difficult theme today
 4 To answer the question 'how are evaluations used' is tantamount to postulating that they are used effectively and that we are able to distinguish precisely what is the result of an evaluation from what is not.
Examples of Use of Evaluations
 1 An example of difficult use of a quality evaluation which the well-disposed decision-maker nevertheless specifically needs.
 2 Two examples of evaluation used to control change.
   Greater parental choice of schools.
   Reform and reorganisation of lower secondary schools.
 3 Examples of evaluations as aids to decision-making.
   Evaluation as the basis for the definition of an ambitious educational policy.
   Adaptation of training courses.
 4 Use of evaluation to enlighten the public, promote awareness and shift the focus of polemics towards better formulated problems.
   From the image of the teaching profession among students to the launching of a recruitment campaign.
   Reading skills of pupils completing elementary school.
 5 Evaluation used to promote progress in evaluation.

Conclusion: Three observations in the form of recommendations.

Summary

INTRODUCTION

Evaluation is too necessary a step, too necessary a process for us to allow it to fall into the hands of the myth-makers or, still worse, to become itself a form of mumbo-jumbo. Accordingly, it seems appropriate first of all to refer briefly to the problem of definition, to give evaluation its rightful place and set a proper value upon it, to explain the difficulties of discussing the use of evaluations in France today and, finally, to illustrate by means of a number of examples various reasons for the use of evaluation in education and methods used, taking due care to deliberate on the sense and validity of the steps taken.

PRELIMINARY REMARKS

Definition

Those in charge of the workshop on the evaluation of educational programmes took the judicious precaution of defining evaluation as 'the assessment and reporting of the process and outcomes of educational programmes in which new methods or changes in organisation or additional resources are introduced' and to include in the scope of evaluation thus delimited 'studies where the purpose is to inform decision-makers on the value and effects of a course, and also studies which are designed to improve a course and give teachers a clearer understanding of factors influencing performance'.

We are therefore close to Daniel L Stufflebeam's definition according to which evaluation is the process whereby useful information on which an appraisal of the possible decisions can be based is delimited, collected and made available.

By putting forward this definition, the organisers of the workshop are in danger of eliminating the question of the evaluation of pupil performances, giving rise to a curious situation in which discussion focuses on evaluation of schools without concerning itself with the very question of knowledge.

It is also necessary to point out that the chosen definition does not eliminate confusion between evaluation and supervision, although they are two different things, nor yet between evaluation and analysis, evaluation and identification and evaluation and research.

These terminological difficulties, which are always present when evaluation is discussed, will not, however, prevent us from adopting a pragmatic approach to the subject.

Giving Evaluation Its Proper Place and Value

Schools did not wait to see evaluation become a key theme before performing its functions and undergoing changes. The changes it undergoes or brings about are so obvious that the question of the school is almost invariably raised from the point of view of what it is, its existence based on knowledge, the imparting of this knowledge, specialists whose role it is to impart it and an institution whose role it is to organise the process.

Jules Ferry in France did not await the birth of the concept of evaluation before deciding that all children should go to school and launching his 'troops', the primary schoolteachers, into all regions and municipalities as part of the fight against illiteracy. It is therefore appropriate to consider the services evaluation can and must render with wisdom and circumspection without minimising its importance and the need it fulfils.

Indeed, when the school was sure of itself, when the values it taught and on which it was based were unanimously acknowledged, there was no attempt to evaluate and still less to ascertain the use of evaluations; it was considered sufficient to monitor the knowledge of pupils, the competence of teachers and the observation of rules in each educational institution.

It is because doubt is being cast on values that questions are asked about what the school evaluates and even the school itself is evaluated; it is not only because democratic principles extend to day-to-day practices, or because public services which are not subject to the laws of the market must nevertheless be accountable, nor yet because of changes in ways of thinking.

Use of Evaluations: a difficult theme today

The question of the use of evaluations is further complicated by the fact that evaluations themselves, their object, their conception, their methods and the way in which they are implemented or utilized are undergoing a process of evolution.

The scope of evaluations is widening, they no longer concern only pupil performances but also systems, establishments, teachers, teacher training and innovations. We no longer evaluate only knowledge and actions but also processes, projects and policies.

The subjects of evaluations are changing: they are no longer concerned solely with acquisitions at a given moment and in terms of deficit; a permanent mechanism is being set up to monitor what young people know without exclusive reference to syllabuses and curricula and in a diachronic perspective. Knowledge of particular subjects is no longer the only object of interest. Attempts are also made to evaluate non-subject-specific competences and pupil attitudes and behaviour: ability to work unsupervised, to handle a new situation, to work alone and in a group, to situate oneself in space and time.

Methods too are evolving:

> indicators are becoming more stable and more subtle and are defined in consultation with all those involved; international harmonisation is being sought;
>
> instruments are becoming more refined and the time lags between the commissioning of the evaluation and delivery of the results are becoming substantially shorter;
>
> relations between evaluators and decision-makers are becoming more fruitful;
>
> ambitions are changing: alongside macroscopic evaluations, more limited evaluations are proliferating and the Ministry is seeking to produce guidelines to help teams in the field, but without any normative pretensions.

We are therefore dealing with a question involving a concept with still incompletely defined contours, which is currently the subject of such intense interest that there is a danger of it becoming a fad, and a rapidly evolving practice.

To Answer the Question 'How are Evaluations Used' is Tantamount to Postulating that They Are Used Effectively and that We can Distinguish Precisely What is the Result of an Evaluation from What is Not.

A superficial observation does not provide the basis for asserting that the evaluations are indeed used. One could even go so far as to suggest without undue impertinence that the links between decisions taken and evaluations made are loose ones.

Can it be claimed that the educational explosion of the 60s was due to the revelation that children with intellectual capacities at least equal to those of high school classes are left in elementary school or rather to a very perceptible growth in the social demand for education, brought about by greater economic wellbeing and increased demands on the part of enterprises?

Can it be said that the change in curricula and directives applied in lower secondary schools is due to an evaluation of the degree of obsolescence of the knowledge conveyed, to an evaluation of the unsuitability of the curricula to the needs and interests of lower secondary pupils, to an evaluation of the correlation between what they know and what they ought to be capable of if they had acquired the knowledge envisaged by the curricula? Or is this change correlation between what they know and what they ought to be capable of if they had acquired the knowledge envisaged by the curricula? Or is this change linked to the need felt by a Minister to assert once more that knowledge and its acquisition by pupils is the most important business of the school?

Can it be maintained that the relaunching of aids to pupils' personal work is based on a precise evaluation of the causes of failure at school? Or was the decision a result of the simple observation that children from privileged backgrounds succeed better, primarily because they receive considerable help at home, and is it a result of the application of plain common sense which suggests that, to succeed, a person must have time to work, a quiet place to study and methodological assistance, mainly supervised or guided studies?

Is the project currently under way to prolong the period of preparation for the baccalaureate to four years rather than three for certain pupils inspired by a genuine evaluation, or is it merely an extension of the principle, already applied in the first years of elementary or lower secondary school, whereby it is preferable to spread courses over a longer period of time rather than to condemn a considerable percentage of pupils to repeat a year, studying the same material with the same methods two years in a row?

In other words, do decision-makers work on the basis of political analyses, general concepts, topical ideas, their personal views of reality, their intuitive perception of the opinion of their fellow citizens, their sense of the way society is moving and of the common good, or do they in fact use the available evaluations which they may themselves have commissioned?

At all events, although the replacement of the term supervision by that of evaluation is not enough to ensure that real developments are discernible, even if changes in terminology do sometimes create an illusion of change, it is nevertheless perfectly possible at this stage to observe different ways in which evaluations are used.

EXAMPLES OF USE OF EVALUATIONS

It would not be appropriate here to follow the example of Stufflebeam and set out a taxonomy in which the various types of use of evaluations, their advantages and disadvantages, their limits and undesirable side-effects are set out in an ordered and exhaustive fashion. My task is to describe in brief a few examples of the use of evaluations. My choice of cases will be guided by the twofold concern to highlight the diversity of uses of evaluations depending on their subjects or the objectives of the users, and to raise a number of questions posed by the use of evaluations.

An Example of Difficult Use of a Quality Evaluation Which the Well-disposed Decision-maker Nevertheless Specifically Needs.

In 1979, the Ministry for Education, perfectly aware of the difficulties of carrying out vast reforms, advised of the relative failure of the implementation of the single lower secondary school and bearing in mind the limits of centralised management of almost 5,000 highly diverse lower secondary schools, sought to 'base the guidance of the system on the educational results of its operation'. Its ambition was 'to know the present situation better in order better to prepare the future'. The idea was to evaluate pupils' knowledge with reference to educational objectives defined by curricula and directives but also with reference to:

the opinions of teachers on the importance of the objectives for the pupils' education;

predictions of success, formulated by the teachers;

teaching conditions.

Educational results were to be correlated with certain individual characteristics, certain components of the social, geographical and economic environment and with factors immanent in the educational system such as size or ability-range of groups, repeating years, etc. Among the other variables taken into account in this huge evaluation were integration into school life, learning of life skills in a community, openness towards the outside world, and preparation for the future (preparation of vocational projects, career guidance).

Sixty state lower secondary schools representing a total of 5,000 were to serve as a sample; 9,300 first-year pupils were to take exams in 1980 (mathematics and French) and 7,600 second- year pupils would be examined in 1982 (6 subjects plus school life). An evaluation based on 8 subjects and school life would be carried out on 6,300 fourth-year pupils in 1984.

Publication of the data alone without commentary required 2,000 pages, which meant that use of the results was bound to prove difficult.

The reform of curricula and directives for lower secondary schools in 1985 constituted an excellent opportunity to make use of this magnum opus.

Having stated that it would be a 'sin against the intellect' not to make use of the results of the educational evaluation carried out in lower secondaries in the work of redesigning curricula, the director in charge came up against difficulties of an epistemological, political and technical nature as daunting as they were diverse.

The design of a curriculum does not depend solely on an evaluation of the extent to which it is applied by teachers, the opinions they form of the relative importance of the various issues to be covered and the ideas to be conveyed or the judgment they reach on the intensity and nature of the difficulties experienced by pupils and an evaluation, however faithful and valid, of the level of acquisition in each subject with reference to precisely defined objectives, cognitive or otherwise.

An educational curriculum must also respect the objectives and logic of each subject and the exigencies inherent in it. The choice of knowledge to be conveyed must take into account not only pupils' potential and tastes and their need for coherence, but also progress in science, the needs of society, the requirements of democracy, the constraints of time, traditions, the current competence of teachers, the existence of powerful public opinion and pressure groups, the construction of Europe and international relations, etc.

Last but not least, technical constraints also have to be contended with.

Such copious and insufficiently synthesised information, the significance of which is not illuminated by the formulation of hypotheses, is difficult to integrate into the work of constructing new curricula. The sheer abundance is daunting and the difficulty of grasping a mass of piecemeal and insufficiently coherent data is further discouragement. In spite of obvious goodwill, it is by no means certain that the new curricula for lower secondary schools undergoing reform owe much to the first major work done on the evaluation (with the exception of mathematics and the physical and natural sciences); it is indeed beyond doubt that much of the available information was insufficiently used or even ignored.

Nevertheless, it is easy to bring to light more subtle and less immediate uses, where evaluation is used less as a basis for taking a decision than to warn those involved, influence public opinion or justify a policy.

The educational evaluation carried out in lower secondary schools shows that part of the disparity in the level of pupil performances is a result of the fact that teachers do not attach the same importance to different items on the syllabus. This observation may be used to justify the very French attitude which sets great store by the syllabus and to justify the implementation policy whereby teachers are given total freedom as to methods and pace, but are required to stick to the syllabus. The demonstration by this same evaluation:

of the fact that pupils, whatever they go on to do later (general studies, vocational training, repetition of the year) fail or succeed in the same areas and the same exercises, albeit in different proportions, and of a broad similarity between results obtained by different groups of pupils (those who go up the next class, those who repeat the year or change their course),

may be used to enlighten public opinion as to the validity of the single lower secondary school, mixed-ability classes and subject sets by ability, provided that each teacher in his class takes account of the children's diversity, adjusts his teaching accordingly and always sticks to what is essential.

By revealing that 6% of 4th year pupils equally successful in all subjects and 12-15% of pupils equally successful in all subjects but one do not currently enter the 5th form, the educational evaluation carried out in lower secondary schools provided the Ministry, a posteriori, with a solid argument for convincing all concerned to work towards the objective of taking 80% of each year up to baccalaureate level.

This last example illustrates the possibilities of using evaluations to test hypotheses which were not formulated at the time of their conception; it is no longer the results of the evaluation which have a retroactive effect on decisions, but rather decisions which have a retroactive effect on the interpretation of the results of evaluations.

As a last comment on this first evaluation, it is curious to note that its results have had no repercussions on the evaluation tools made available to teachers and on the way applied research in differentiated subject-based teaching methods is conducted.

Admittedly, the use of evaluation depends on clarity of results, simplicity of presentation, the degree to which they synthesise data and the relevance of the questions which shed light on the problems posed by the decision-maker, but it also depends on adequate matching of results obtained and measures implemented by those responsible for making decisions.

Two Examples of Evaluation Used to Control Change
Greater parental choice of schools
The aspiration of the French to more freedom in the organisation of their day-to-day life, the store set by education in a context of unemployment and technological upheaval, the extension of consumer attitudes to the field of education and political willingness to give the citizen broad powers of decision led the Ministry of Education to launch in 1982 an experiment in more flexible 'sectorisation'. Sectorisation consists in obliging a family to send its child to the lower secondary school in the geographical 'sector' in which the family resides.

Responsibility for observing the conditions and consequences of implementing a procedure of allocation of pupils to lower secondary schools which gave families the choice between several state establishments was assigned to the Inspectorate General and the econometrics laboratory of the Ecole Polytechnique.

For the Ministry, the idea was to use the results of an evaluation to steer a change made difficult by the fact that any policy reversal or refusal to apply the new system across the board was likely to give rise to strong public reaction.

The evaluation, carried out in 1987, brought to light a number of phenomena:

> the rate of requests to change school was relatively stable in both spatial and temporal terms: 10%;
>
> the rate of compliance with requests was high, averaging 70%, but varied considerably depending on the capacities of attractive establishments;
>
> a quarter of lower secondary schools gained pupils, a quarter lost some;
>
> highly popular or popular schools gained further positive attributes from the point of view of staff composition, courses offered and the social composition of the school population, whereas highly unpopular or unpopular schools experienced the reverse;
>
> the most privileged socio-professional categories benefited most from these measures; they were at once better informed and more demanding, they were able to present arguments more acceptable to the institution and the underlying reason for the request to change schools was mostly of an evaluative nature (choice of a school with a better reputation) than a functional one (choice of a school more easily accessible from the parents' place of work, etc);
>
> whatever the socio-professional category of applicants, whatever the reasons for the request, a change of establishment always meant that the pupil attended a school with attributes superior to those of the establishment he would normally have attended.

The non-confidential character of this evaluation, the involvement of different bodies, the close association between decision-makers and evaluators and the continuity of the evaluation despite political changes are worth emphasising. It should also be noted that this type of evaluation leads a decision-maker to ask new questions or formulate problems differently. Here, the problem was how to reconcile greater freedom of choice and the desire for greater equality.

Reform of lower secondary schools
A brief comparison between the way evaluation was used when the single lower secondary school was introduced in application of the 1975 Act and during the reform process launched by a ministerial declaration in 1983 will bring to light a number of developments, help us to understand their origin and to learn a number of useful lessons. The arrangements selected for implementing a change largely determine the nature of possible evaluations and their use.

The 1975 Educational Reform Act which set up the single (comprehensive) lower secondary school created the need to supervise its application, not to evaluate the appropriateness of the decisions taken. Only a crisis situation led to a shift from supervision towards evaluation. In the year 1979/80, the Inspectorate General spoke in a report, notorious despite its confidential nature, of 'degeneration of reform, demotivation and passivity which augur a complete collapse of all the ambitions proclaimed in 1975'. It was not until 1982/83 that, helped by a major political change, this evaluation was really used and recommendations concerning 'encouragement of heads of schools to acquire a taste and capacity for initiative' taken into consideration.

It is plain that in a situation of reform by legislative means, imposed from above, evaluation is not sought until serious difficulties arise and is only used or usable after a very long period of reflection. It is also apparent in the present case that the use of the evaluation was very partial, particularly since the analyses and proposals were no longer necessarily in keeping with the prevailing mood, situation and ambitions. For example, comments in the report cited, such as the statement that 'it would be illusory to believe that autonomy (of establishments) would turn out to be miraculously synonymous with innovative policy or progress' or on the advisability of reintroducing streaming in certain cases, fell on deaf ears.

In the wake of this experience there emerged from 1986/87 onwards a desire to study the implementation of the conditions of reform; the current reform of lower secondary schools was neither launched by legislation nor imposed from above, but, as it were, proposed as a way out of a blind alley and progressively implemented by a process of negotiation, cultivation of responsibility and decentralisation of decision-making which incorporated an evaluation procedure in its very conception.

In such circumstances, national, regional or local evaluations are immediately implemented; they are regularly, effectively used and allow for rapid and numerous adjustments.

A comparative study of the four national evaluation reports drawn up by the Inspectorate General and the annual circulars issued at the beginning of the school year on the reform of lower secondary schools clearly shows that available information was used almost meticulously to adjust decisions to difficulties and remedy distortions or the unwanted side-effects observed.

It is in response to the evaluations that the circulars state that:

ability-based subject sets should now be considered as no more than one way of dealing with mixed-ability groups and should concern only part of the timetable in three subjects in order to avoid a return to streaming;

directors of education may accept only such establishment plans which forgo generous or utopian considerations, are based on a detailed analysis of the situation and include strict programming;

observation courses (first and second year) over three years may be mounted to resolve problems of excessive variation in ability.

For all that, the situation has not become idyllic; national evaluations too often remain macroscopic and fail to incorporate sufficient variables, and the decision-maker does not use all the data available, nor remedy all the malfunctions brought to light. For example, ambiguities remain as regards flexible time management or the definition of teachers' obligations and duties. Nevertheless, we would assert that failure to take certain aspects of proposals into account disqualifies neither the evaluation nor the evaluator, nor yet the decision-maker; the act of evaluation does not dispense anyone from exercising his judgment, having a sense of timing and exercising his administrative or political responsibility.

Examples of Evaluations as Aids to Decision-making

Evaluations as the basis for the definition of an ambitious educational policy
The use made of the work carried out by the Bureau d'information et de prevision economique (Economic Information and Forecasting Office) and the Haut Comité Education Economie (High Committee on Education and Economics) on the evaluation of quantitative and qualitative employment needs in the year 2000 is a particularly interesting illustration of the way in which evaluation can act as an aid to decision-making.

In response to a commission assigned to them by the Ministry in 1984, the two above-mentioned bodies demonstrated the need for a dramatic change in the distribution of skills in the workforce between now and the year 2000 and showed that efforts to raise the level of initial training for the generations born from 1980 onwards would have to be all the greater since the low level of skills in the present working population would still be a serious handicap in the year 2000. Indeed, a large proportion of the population currently at work would remain in the year 2000 and in spite of continuous and in-service training, there would have been little improvement in the overall level of skills.

Obviously, the Ministry did not commission an analysis of this kind and instigate an evaluation of needs without first designing a project for upgrading schools and training, but it was able to use the results to launch a very ambitious project which has considerable support today: to ensure that 80% of each year reach baccalaureate level in the year 2000 and to establish a new qualification: the vocational baccalaureate, a diploma vital to the credibility of the upgrading of technological training.

It was on the basis of this first evaluation and the decisions which it at least facilitated that more sophisticated plans could be conceived and implemented. The plan for the future of education is obviously a result of the strongly motivating effect of the campaign to ensure that 80% of each year reach baccalaureate level.

We thus see over and over again in reality and within one country a necessary cycle in which an evaluation phase precedes a decision-making phase which is then followed by a phase of still more complex and more sophisticated evaluation.

Adaptation of training

Among the many examples of evaluation as an aid to decision-making, we may take the role played by the surveys carried out by the Centre d'Etudes et de Recherche sur les Qualifications (CEREQ) (Skills, Study and Research Centre) in the very rapid and thorough modernisation of technical education diplomas. These surveys concern changes in tasks, intellectual requirements, competences, levels of skill and changes in requirements depending on the type of company and geographical location. The work carried out by joint consultative committees comprising representatives of professional organisations and trade unions and national education officials would not have led to appropriate and rational decisions if it had not been for the undoubted quality of the CEREQ evaluations and surveys.

For instance, this body's demonstration that poor adjustment in the chemical sector between the 'products' of the education system, who mainly gravitate towards laboratory jobs, and the needs of companies, which are seeking manufacturing technicians, helped to bring about the creation of a vocational baccalaureate oriented towards industrial manufacturing and an update of workers' diplomas.

Naturally, this presentation is a simplistic one, as its intention is simply to highlight the creation of institutional links between evaluation and decision-making.

Use of Evaluation to Enlighten the Public, Promote Awareness and Shift the Focus of Polemics towards Better Formulated Problems.

From the image of the teaching profession among students to the launching of a recruitment campaign

Study of professional images is nothing new; nowadays it is a determining factor in all forms of theoretical and practical career guidance. What is new, and even revolutionary, is the use of such studies by the state education system to launch a recruitment campaign. Admittedly, given the shortage of applications, the state education system will have to step up its recruitment rate considerably, as it will have to take on over 300,000 new teachers in the next twelve years.

But what image do students have of this career which is said to be the finest of all? A survey commissioned by the Direction de l'évaluation et de la prospective (Directorate of Forward Planning and Evaluation) provides part of the answer. Students are relatively well informed about the conditions of access even if they over-estimate the level of diploma required for application; however, they underestimate their chances of success in the competitive examinations. They think of the teaching profession as conferring considerable advantages (holidays, protection) but also as stressful and exercised in an ill-adapted system. Students are not particularly attracted to teaching as such, but prefer the job of a secondary school teacher who conveys knowledge to that of a primary school teacher, who is perceived as playing the most important role and forming an emotional relationship with pupils but has the lowest status.

One of the strictly practical problems of the recruitment campaign will be to take this image into account without offending either teachers or parents of pupils.

How can one avoid thinking about the necessary evaluation of this campaign? What impact will it have on potential candidates and on public opinion? Will the need for evaluation ever be satisfied?

Reading skills of pupils completing elementary school
The topicality of the highly motivating theme of bringing 80% of a given year up to baccalaureate level, and subjects such as illiteracy or a fall in school standards give rise to sterile polemics and create a need for evaluation to restore calm. It is easy to imagine that, to reach baccalaureate level, it is better to enter lower secondary school with an adequate command of the fundamental mechanisms. An evaluation of the standard of reading skills among children leaving elementary school was therefore launched in 1987.

This evaluation reveals a wide range of levels and shows in particular that although three quarters of the pupils understand broadly a text read, only half of them read it thoroughly. Success at the lower secondary schools requires that pupils should be capable of reading a text thoroughly. The fairly wide dissemination of the results of this survey was intended both to enlighten the public and to motivate all those concerned to concentrate on reading. Although there has indeed been growing interest in reading and one parents' federation launched this academic year the idea of a 'reading plan', a sort of crusade for all concerned, there is also a noticeable increase in confusion in the minds of the French people: they used to believe that 20% of children did not know how to read, which did not make much sense; today they think the figure is 50%, which is ridiculous.

That is a curious and counter-productive effect of the use of the results of an evaluation designed to instil rationality into a necessary debate and to create dynamism focusing on the school.

Evaluation Used to Promote Progress in Evaluation
One rather sophisticated use of evaluation is to evaluate the level of awareness of the need for evaluation or the degree of mastery of evaluation procedures of a particular category of staff with a view to developing an evaluative attitude or improving evaluation skills.

An evaluation of this type was carried out among heads of schools (lower secondary and upper secondary schools). The object was to evaluate the extent to which they carried out internal evaluations to help them conduct their establishments by taking account of the problems arising in them and the results of the actions or decisions they took. A further aim was to identify their attitudes to external evaluation.

This work, carried out in 1987 by the General Inspectorate of Schools, demonstrated that one head out of two was anxious to gain an objective picture of the phenomena where action was needed by setting up what might be called a 'control panel'. It should be pointed out that heads of schools who receive from the regional departments a compendium of indicators concerning their schools often claim that they never refer to this incomprehensible technocratic tool. In fact, a significantly greater proportion of heads of schools who receive this compendium construct a 'control panel' of their own. It is thus fair to say that the mere fact of disseminating 'government indicators' surreptitiously induces an evaluative attitude.

Another interesting result of this evaluation was to show that most heads of schools were willing to comply with an evaluative request provided there was no confusion between hierarchical supervision - which was not rejected - internal evaluation and external evaluation. Furthermore, the educational virtues of this evaluation are clear: the schools evaluated concern themselves more with evaluation than do other establishments.

I am aware of the anecdotal aspect of this paper; my intention was to avoid taking refuge in theoretical reflection or launching into a normative construction beyond my capacity to complete.

More of a farmer than an agronomist, I have hereby referred very freely to the evaluations whose results have come to my notice and commented on their use. I hope that some will find the information provided useful, and that I shall be forgiven for choosing simplicity although I am aware that 'what is simple is false' and that 'what is not is useless' (Paul Valery).

CONCLUSION

By way of conclusion, I have three observations to make.

It seems important that we should develop simultaneously evaluations conducted locally and those conducted at national level. In view of the recent setting up by the French Ministry of a directorate of evaluation and forward planning, it is worth pointing out the need to leave a considerable area of freedom as regards evaluation and the use made of evaluations at local level. It is indeed easier and more effective to use evaluations locally, as they are generally less political in character and because they allow those directly affected to be taken to be more closely involved in the conclusions to be drawn and the decisions to be taken.

It is also important to stress the need to use different evaluators who do not have the same type of relations with the decision-makers. The system should provide itself with a considerable evaluative capacity and competence but it must also call in outside assistance and promote initiatives in the choice of themes. What is true for research is also true for evaluation.

Finally, I would point out the usefulness and effectiveness of solicited evaluation and self-evaluation. The current operation of the National

Committee for the Evaluation of Universities is exemplary in this respect. I shall not resist the temptation to cite the case of a university which, having asked to be evaluated, made changes on such a scale after the experts' first visit that they were obliged to start their work all over again. Is it conceivable that the university would have used the evaluation with such ardour if it had been imposed upon it from outside?

SUMMARY

Evaluation is too necessary for the improvement of the operation and performance of the school for us to run the risk of reducing it to a fad. We must therefore take care: to define precisely what we understand by evaluation, and give it its proper place by removing all elements of myth attaching to it and ensuring that it does not degenerate into mumbo-jumbo; to take into account the very rapid and recent development of its concepts and practices and not deny the difficulty of identifying the consequences of its use.

References to several evaluations carried out in France and selected because of the diversity of their object and objectives:

educational evaluation in lower secondary schools;

evaluation of greater parental choice of school;

evaluation of the reform and subsequent reorganisation of lower secondary schools;

evaluation of the needs for skills in the year 2000;

evaluation of the extent to which training is adapted to jobs;

the image of the teaching profession among students;

evaluation of reading skills of children completing elementary schools;

evaluation of the abilities of heads of schools as regards evaluation;

serve to illustrate some of the ways of using evaluation, and deriving benefit from the results, and to show that significant progress has been made in these areas.

Evaluations are not only used to take or justify decisions, control changes and regulate action, but also to enlighten the public, arouse awareness, alter behaviour, motivate the participants and add depth to debate. It is found, although the evidence is not adduced here, that the use of evaluations is easier and more effective when they are included from the outset in a process of concerted change, when they are instigated before situations decline to a marked extent, when they involve those concerned and are conceived at the level at which they are to be used, when they are solicited and when the time-lag between their commissioning and the delivery of results is not too long.

Nowadays, it is vital for the school to be aware and to give account of itself if it is to have a real and enduring existence. This means that the school has a duty to perform its task more effectively, at optimum costs, however high that may be, and to see to it that its work does not pass unnoticed.

HOW ARE EVALUATIONS USED?
List of questions

1. What studies can be produced on the impact of evaluations?

2. Are the evaluations which have been carried out useful and usable?

3. Who uses evaluations: institutions or users?

4. What are evaluations currently most often used for in different countries?

5. To what extent should evaluations be public? Why? How?

6. Are there perceptible developments in the use of evaluations? If so, what are they and what has caused them? How can these developments be sustained or speeded up?

7. What are the properties inherent in the most and best used evaluations?

8. What factors external to evaluations favour their use (commissioning agent, nature of commission, nature of relationship between the evaluation and its use)?

9. What are the reasons most often given for not using evaluations?

10. At what levels (national, regional, local) do evaluations seem most easily usable?

11. What unwanted side effects have been or may be caused by the use of evaluations?

12 Should we try to draw up directives on the use of evaluations and if so why?

13 Should we envisage training in the use of evaluation for those who commission them, evaluators themselves and users of evaluations?

References
STUFFLEBEAM, D. (1980) *L'évaluation en éducation*. Quebec: NHP.

6
The Uses of Evaluation

Robert S Long
Oxfordshire County Council Education Department,
England

The County Council is a Local Education Authority (LEA), with responsibility including 247 primary schools and 47 secondary schools, employing 4000 teachers. It is a mix of urban and rural areas, generally prosperous.

PREAMBLE
The culture and implicit principles of the LEA inform and are reflected in the evaluation activities. At the centre is the individual institution, not the LEA. A major LEA role is to be responsive to institutional need, managing resources accordingly. We hold to the view that through the development of the reflective teacher and the reflective school, even more effective learning for pupils will ensue. This permeates prioritising and decision-making, for example in relation to in-service training (INSET) budgets, the structure of projects which the LEA supports, and the roles of LEA personnel.

THE FIRST ROUND OF THE OXFORDSHIRE SCHOOL SELF-EVALUATION PROGRAMME
Background to the Programme
Towards the end of 1978 the Chief Education Officer initiated discussions, through working parties representing the various teacher interests and officers and advisers in the Education Department, on the issue of evaluation of schools.

The discussions were timely, for two reasons. Firstly there was the feeling, expressed both at national and at local levels, that schools should be seen to be accountable to a wider community. Secondly it was clear that the national and local resources available to education would at best not increase, and that any initiatives aimed at further improving the quality of learning, teaching and pupil achievement would need to start from a critical analysis of existing practice.

A number of LEAs throughout the country were engaged to work on the same theme. Some eventually recast the role of their advisers into that of inspectors; others increased their central staff in order to step up external influences on schools; a few devised schemes through which schools looked more formally at their own performance, either with or without external input. Oxfordshire was one of the latter, and on 14 June 1979 a system of schools evaluation with two components, one mainly internal and one mainly external, was approved by the Education Committee and was initiated in the 1979-80 academic year. One component of the scheme was the publication of a booklet for all teachers, called 'Starting Points in Self-evaluation'. Teachers and advisers across the county had contributed ideas and comments at drafting stages, and the booklet had two purposes, described in its foreword, namely to be:

(a) an aid to teachers, individually or collectively, and to schools in examining the value of what they do;

(b) a starting point for discussion and further questioning whenever a school as a whole, or a department within a school, considers it appropriate to take stock of what it is achieving.

The other component of the Oxfordshire scheme, which it is thought was unique at that time, was the requirement that schools should produce a report once every four years for the Schools' Sub-committee (County Councillors and Members), who established a Panel to receive the reports and to discuss them with Headteachers.

Thus Oxfordshire set out on a new path without the benefit of guidance or instruction from other areas or organisations. It is therefore a tribute to the work and commitment of our teachers, Headteachers and Members, to the principle of school self-evaluation and their willingness to experiment with approaches to it, that the majority of those who have been consulted in preparation for this paper are firmly in favour of the county-wide school self-evaluation scheme, subject to improvements which are reflected in the second round.

The First Report Cycle In Practice
Procedure and Time Scale
Most schools have taken between six months and a year to review their statements of aims and objectives, to gather facts, opinions and observations on which to base their self-evaluation, to hold evaluative discussions and to write their school report. Primary schools are recommended to produce not more than twenty pages and secondary schools not more than sixty; many

produce much more. Once the document has been typed and reproduced it is presented to the Governors, who meet to discuss it, and to provide a commentary of their own if they wish. In the term following the presentation to Governors, the report is discussed by the Evaluation Panel. The Head, and more recently the Chairman of Governors also, is invited to attend the Panel meeting, and in most cases both do so. The Chief Education Officer or a representative, together with the appropriate Area Officer and if possible an Adviser, are also present. The local County Councillor is invited. Soon after the pilot projects were received, a further stage began for secondary schools. For this, a team of three or more Officers/Advisers visit the school for several hours' discussion with the Head and other senior staff to discuss further directions and, where appropriate, to agree on support which the LEA can provide for achieving goals. The agenda for this meeting includes items requested by the school and items raised by Officers. An informal note to record the meeting is then sent to the Head from the Education Department. In the Autumn of 1983, a similar personal follow-up procedure was instituted for primary schools and special schools, normally involving the Area Education Officer and the local Adviser and replacing the purely written formal response.

The interval from the first decisions in the school on the process of evaluation to the professional follow-up meeting in the school can be two years or more, and for half of that time the process may not be visible to most of the teachers in the school. Sometimes they think that nothing is happening as far as their report is concerned, though they themselves, having decided on their future directions, will be involved in developing them so far as they are able.

Panel Meetings
By the end of the first cycle the Panel had met almost 100 times and discussed reports from over 250 schools. The time allocated for each school varied from one to one and a half hours, depending on the size of the school. The discussion always began with information - giving, confidential comments from the Panel member who had visited the schools. The Head and Chairman of Governors then joined the meeting, the head being asked initially to highlight key issues in each section. Such was the expertise and experience of the Panel that the formality of the setting was usually overcome and many Heads felt able to speak freely with the Panel about the problems, achievements and future plans of their schools.

Evaluation of the School Self-Evaluation Scheme
Objectives
The major purposes of evaluating schools are:
  (a) to contribute to the fullest possible pupil achievement through identifying possible further improvements for the quality of learning and teaching and the management of the school;

  (b) to demonstrate accountability to the resource-providing community (Local and Central Government).

The school *self*-evaluation scheme, such as that pioneered in Oxfordshire, attempts to do this by making the school responsible for accounting for itself and by making full use of the professional expertise which exists within the institution, both for goal-setting, in consultation with the local community, and for development based on reflecting on performance. An institution which is confidently self-evaluative is able to request and make good use of external contributions such as HMI Reports, local Adviser consultation, parent/governor participation, without destroying its own command of the evaluative process. It is fundamental to any school self-evaluation scheme that all directly concerned with the school have a view of the performance of that school which is worth noting, and that it is the responsibility of the Head, with the assistance of staff and Governors at minimum, to collect and deliberate upon all the available indicators of performance, whether subjective (ie opinions of internal or external observers or participants' personal judgments) or objective (ie statistical data).

Obtaining Evidence of Achievement of Objectives
The objective of *demonstrating accountability* must be judged by the processes which are set up to achieve it. In the Oxfordshire scheme the school, in collaboration with its governing body representing the local but non-funding community, accounts for itself to the County Council as both employer and provider of resources, either on its own account or on behalf of Central Government. If all parties carry out their part in the programme, then this objective is met.

The *educational* objective is demonstrated far less easily. A simplistic view is to imagine that one can measure improvement in achievement in a sufficiently precise way over a defined period of time and then confidently attribute that improvement to a specific process such as school self-evaluation. That is not to say that one may never hazard a good guess about the effect of one set of actions on another set of indicators. Professionals and politicians alike do this constantly. It is self-evident, however, that even where improvement can be demonstrated against known criteria and a known base-line, that it is still a matter of opinion as to what exactly has contributed to it. It is therefore essential to recognise that even if we had been engaged in this programme for four or five cycles instead of nearly one, and even if we had begun with a perfect base-line description of the state of education in every single school, we would still be relying on our individual and collective *subjective* judgments to help us to decide whether the educational objective was being met, or how to improve our collective performance in meeting it.

THE SECOND ROUND OF THE OXFORDSHIRE SCHOOL SELF-EVALUATION SCHEME

The First Cycle

The first cycle of school self-evaluation in Oxfordshire gave schools the opportunity to draw together reflections on a broad range of their life and work. This process formalised the critical reviewing which was already a feature of many schools and allowed schools to take stock and to identify future directions. The report produced at the end of the process provided a useful focus for discussions with Governors and elected Members (through the Schools' Evaluation Panel).

The Second Cycle

The second cycle has developed from the first. Schools are asked to reflect on three broad issues identified by the LEA and on two issues which they identify themselves. The report is hence less all-embracing than in the first cycle, but does allow detailed review of some features. The range of factors in the present context, not least being the experience of the first cycle, means that schools do not *start* evaluating when they come to the second cycle.

The LEA-nominated topics are:
- (a) Continuity through and between areas of curriculum and on transfer between classes and schools;

- (b) Issues relating to prejudice and equal opportunity;

- (c) The schools' partnership with parents and its work alongside the local community.

All Oxfordshire schools are engaged in continuing review, reflection, and consequent development. This points to an important feature of the second cycle: that schools will generally link the requirements into their own pattern of review and development, harnessing for their already agreed purposes and adapting where necessary. At the core is the knowledge that good development derives from informed reflection, supported by appropriate resources and opportunities for growth.

Organisation

The reporting sequence of the whole cycle runs from 1987 to 1992. Schools in the same partnership (primary and linked secondary) are asked to report in the same term. This allows coordinated support and follow-up. In addition, it enables identification of trends and issues across a group of schools.

Generally, the process starts at least a year before the report is to be presented. There are four elements:

(a) **Preparation** - schools develop plans for managing the process and ways of evaluating. This involves close linking with advisers and officers. The plans incorporate such of the support resources as the schools decides and identify the schools' chosen issues;

(b) **Process** - a term or more in which a range of approaches may be used for evaluating;

(c) **Reporting** - the completing of the report, its passage through a number of drafts, presentation to Governors, and submission to the Evaluation Panel. The school-based meeting of the Evaluation Panel is then followed by review of the partnership group's reports and meetings at the full Evaluation Panel;

(d) **Follow-up** - a report is made by the Evaluation Panel which is discussed by Schools' Sub-comittee. Advisers and Officers plan follow-up with the school.

The Process - Support and Resources

In drawing up their plans, schools work closely with their linked Advisers. The Adviser has two functions in this respect: first, to provide general support and advice, and secondly to act as 'broker' linking in to the school, where requested, the support resources available in the LEA.

The preparation stage includes a meeting for all partnership schools in which resources and possibilities are considered. These include:

(a) **Continuity:** Adviser guidance, general and specialist;

(b) **Prejudice and Equal Opportunities:** Equal Opportunities Advisory Teacher, Multi-cultural Centre Team, Development Unit;

(c) **Parents and Community:** The parental involvement group team of Advisory Teachers.

In relation to these and areas of the school's own choice, it is also possible to involve Higher Education Staff on a consultancy basis. In addition, some supply staffing is available to help teachers in their evaluating: for example, observing each other's classes as a way of looking at continuity. Advisers with relevant specialisms and Advisory Teams (for example, Science and Mathematics) can also be consulted. Some schools have found it helpful to involve members of the wider community - for example, industrialists.

With this substantial range of resources, it is possible to refine and develop useful ways of looking. Clearly, it may not be possible for each school to evaluate all five areas in similar depth. Within partnerships, schools can profitably link for some aspects; in particular, when looking at the primary/secondary aspect of continuity.

Comment on the Second Round

A few tentative comments are possible, bearing in mind that only about 25% of the institutions have reported.

(i) The three LEA strands have been helpful in focusing on areas for development. They have led to significant change during the process of self-evaluation, and to some action programmes following the reporting;

(ii) The LEA has invested more resources to support schools, on request, in the self-evaluation process. Particularly where these resources have been used, there has been a significant shift from description to evaluation;

(iii) Issues remain about the tension between self-evaluation and accountability.

'OTHER' EVALUATION

The period of institutional self-evaluation in Oxfordshire has been complemented by strategies at local and national level to achieve change through the creation of projects with specific foci: for example increasing technical and vocational learning, improving home-school links (parents as partners), developing study skills. In Oxfordshire we have at least thirty such projects. These projects generally carry with them evaluation requirements which usually mean the commissioning of 'external' evaluation. Hence, running alongside our self-evaluation programme we have a range of other evaluation activities and demands. We have been concerned that project evaluation might

    (a)   lead to evaluation overload;

    (b)   conflict with self-evaluation principles.

Hence we have agreed a set of commissioned evaluation principles which create a framework for this work.

Evaluation principles for commissioned evaluation

1. Evaluation should derive from or complement teachers' and institutions' own self-evaluation.

2. It should be formative and summative.

3. The style and nature of evaluation should be negotiated between the evaluators and those nominated by the LEA who have appropriate involvement in that which is being evaluated. The negotiation should include consideration of confidentiality and reporting.

4. Criteria should, wherever possible, focus on quality of learning as well as matters such as management and teacher perceptions.

5. Evaluation should incorporate resource analysis and replication implications.

6. Evaluation should utilize centrally-held national and local information, eg re staffing, curriculum, examination results, in order to reduce the demands on institutions.

7   Illuminative strategies should be used as well as quantitative/statistical.

INSTITUTIONAL ACCREDITATION
In Oxfordshire, most pupils who leave full-time education take with them a Record of Achievement. This is a summary document which reflects a wide range of each individual's achievement. It is based on guided self-assessment. Schools/colleges are empowered to issue these Records by an accreditation process which involves demonstrating that certain principles about reviewing, recording and reporting are being addressed.

NEW DEVELOPMENTS
The English system is undergoing substantial change. New legislation in England and Wales makes specific demands on LEAs to monitor/inspect educational provision. At the same time it is designed to ensure that control of resources and policy rests at institutional level. It focuses significantly on the creation of performance indicator data as a means of institutional evaluation.

Perhaps surprisingly, this approach reinforces the growth in evaluation in Oxfordshire during the last ten years. The institutional self-referential model fits with these requirements. The LEA, in its support role, is currently engaged in:

1   Establishing a menu/catalogue of performance indicators, in partnership with institutions, which will include indicators required by:
(i) the institutions - teachers, parents, governors and the wider community;
(ii) institutional accreditation;
(iii) the LEA;
(iv) projects;
(v) central government.

2   Exploring the concept of 'validating context'. The traditional inspectorial model is not effective.

3   Developing evaluation guidelines linked to each indicator.

4   Developing institutional plans for using appropriate indicators.

5   Re-negotiating commissioned evaluation to ensure that it is enveloped within this pattern.

'EVALUATION NOW'
I think we are shifting towards a new model/set of parameters for evaluation.

It will be institution-based as well as focused. It will depend on evaluation by teachers and heads of institutions.

It will incorporate others as:
(a) 'critical friends' to support the institution's review - who will be engaged by the institution;

(b) support for developing ways of evaluating.

I see the role of current 'evaluators' as linking to (a) and (b). The needs for discrete evaluations for 'projects' will change, as their needs are reflected in the performance indicator catalogue.

NATIONAL AND LOCAL EVALUATION
Within the perspective of this model, there remains the need for national and local/regional evaluation. The model, deriving from self-evaluation, needs expanding from the institution to the LEA to the national. It will require substantial change and will affect the nature of evaluation contracts beyond the institution.

OTHER THOUGHTS
1   'Evaluation' has developed as a concept underpinning a range of methods and activities, often necessarily at some distance from the learning of pupils. The 'industry' has grown from patterns of thought and practice within the social sciences. Methodology may have been precise but has tended to be leisurely. The pace of change means that evaluation available two years later is frequently irrelevant ('We've done it'). Hence we need to explore new models.

2   The link between 'evaluation', 'monitoring' and inspection needs to be explored.

3   Who are the evaluators? Increasingly, there is a broadening range: the Government - the University - the LEA - the governors - the parents - the pupils.

OVERVIEW

Oxfordshire LEA is committed to the concept of supported self-evaluation. This is linked to the idea of 'monitoring support'. It starts from a self-referential base at institutional level (and within that at individual teacher level). I think we can incorporate other, proper demands within that context. We need to use the perceptions of others, outside the institution, including those with professional 'evaluation' expertise. In particular, we have a responsibility to enable institutions and their teachers to refine their own reflection. We have not employed a 'hard' model which makes *direct* links between resource allocation and evaluation, or policy formulation and evaluation. We could be challenged in that our approach is 'osmotic', non-directive...It is less easy to define, fits less well into conference presentations, but we think it works. The thrust of this paper should demonstrate why I think we need to review the notion of 'evaluations' if we start from the institution.

GROUP WORK TOPICS
The use of self-evaluation
1   The viability of the institutional self-evaluation model.
2   The role of other evaluators.
3   The relationship of institutional self-evaluation to regional and national evaluation.
4   Conceptual definitions: evaluation, monitoring, review, inspection.

Evaluation of Educational Programmes in Austria

Dr Friedrich Weyermüller
Director of the Institute for Education of the Tyrol, Innsbruck

In Austria, compulsory schooling essentially takes place in 'Allgemeinbildende Pflichtschulen' (general compulsory schools), covering primary (Volksschule) and upper primary/lower secondary (Hauptschule) education and 'Allgemeinbildende Höheree Schulen' (secondary general schools) covering lower secondary education. This report presents a brief survey of the results of evaluations - completed or about to be - carried out in the context of specialised research projects.

1. *Pädagogisches Institut des Landes Tirol in Innsbruck (Weyermüller)*
   (Institute for education of the land of Tyrol, Innsbruck)
   Special teaching - rehabilitation of mentally handicapped children in an all-day programme, with a 48-minute video presentation;

   A school for children between 10 and 14 years old - the school in the countryside.

2. *Zentrum für Schulversuche und Schulentwicklung in Graz (Petri)*
   (Centre for school experiments and school development, Graz)
   Course prototype *Ticket to Britain*;

   Pilot project *Learning to work in a group*;

   Co-operative learning - methods, strategies, approaches.

3. *Bundesministerium für Unterricht, Kunst und Sport in Wien (Wolf)*
   (Federal Ministry of Education, the Arts and Sport, Vienna)
   Testing of primary school curricula;

   Testing of teaching methods at primary level.

In view of the limited time and space at my disposal, I shall restrict myself to introducing the first four subjects. Those of you who would like to become acquainted with the other results are invited to contact the individuals and institutions mentioned at the end of the text, who would be delighted to provide you with further information.

PROBLEMS OF REHABILITATION OF MENTALLY HANDICAPPED CHILDREN IN AN ALL-DAY PROGRAMME

For several years now, a pilot project has been under way in Lienz, the purpose of which is to put forward rehabilitation measures for mentally handicapped persons considered to be teachable but not able to attend a normal school, for whom virtually no systematic support has been provided up to now.

The rehabilitation programmed applied, which covers the entire day, involves all aspects of practical living likely to help each child discover a personal identity. The model adopted relieves the mother of a large number of tasks whilst at the same time maintaining the child's family links, and thereby helps to improve the psycho-social conditions of the family as a whole. The decision to expose a child so dependent upon the protection of others to the school environment is not always an easy one. A handicap of this kind always affects the entire personality and any rehabilitation geared to such a child must therefore be comprehensive. The aim is to stimulate communicative and active faculties without neglecting the child's emotional needs. Guidance in the immediate surroundings, the awakening of interests which will help the child discover genuine recreational pastimes, a maximum degree of independence with a view to an autonomous life in the future and the ability to pursue a group activity all have to be developed from the outset by means of play.

It is very unusual to see such children perform spontaneous acts. Most of their reactions are the result of rehabilitation measures carried out systematically over many years. Everything these children acquire in this way must have its use in everyday life.

It is important to concentrate equally on all major areas. It may be necessary to place greater emphasis on a particular activity at a given moment, but care must always be taken to ensure that the support measures are linked together and are present throughout the day. Each capacity and faculty must be developed gradually by a series of small steps and should then be practised in every possible and imaginable situation. Specific measures geared to everyday life and involving various types of materials and equipment are particularly appropriate for stimulating and strengthening the individual's self-reliance and independence.

It is a long and arduous road which must be travelled day after day, paying careful attention to every step. Within an educational framework designed to prepare these children for the practical aspects of life, it is imperative to arrange activities outside the school: the children go shopping, go to the post office or the station, or go for a walk like the group of children in the final class. The purpose of this group outing is partly to improve the way handicapped children relate to themselves and their environment and partly to educate the outside world by teaching it to accept these children and their difference.

Evaluation mechanism
The evaluation of the project 'rehabilitation of mentally handicapped children by an all-day programme' follows the formative principle, that is to say data and experience collected on a continuous basis are immediately processed and translated into practical measures at regular meetings of the team in charge of the project (project leader, doctor, therapist, teachers and parents). The measures proposed are then checked to ascertain how effective they are, and maintained, modified or stopped, depending on whether or not they further the achievement of the desired objectives. One essential element in the evaluation process is the exchange of experiences between all those involved in the project - with the exception of the children. This takes the form of observations, analyses, reports of personal experiences and presentation of objective results of medical or psycho-pedagogical examinations which can then be processed qualitatively or quantitatively and serve to guide the subsequent activity of the medical, psychological and educational staff.

A SCHOOL FOR CHILDREN BETWEEN 10 AND 14 YEARS OLD - THE SCHOOL IN THE COUNTRYSIDE

In the course of history, the countryside has undergone numerous social changes which have been to its detriment, so that it is now a disadvantaged environment. Periods of general economic crisis in particular accentuate these handicaps and further aggravate the difficult situation of rural areas. The survival problems of small industries are reflected by loss of jobs, flight from the land or at least costly and time-consuming periodic migrations. Over the past decades, these general trends have also had repercussions on schools. One result has been the creation of schools in regional centres designed to cater for the school-age population of the surrounding areas.

The concentration of schoolchildren in these central establishments has certainly attenuated inequalities of opportunity, but at the same time it has brought about a profound change in the living structures of rural families and villages. In the early morning, the children are collected by a bus which takes them to a distant town. If their timetable includes afternoon lessons, they will not go back for lunch with the family and will not return to their families and villages until late afternoon or nightfall in the wintertime. For these children, the equality of opportunity acquired in the town goes hand-in-hand with a loosening of ties with their familiar environment.

In order to perform its role as a place of education and training which prepares the child and adolescent for all aspects of life, the school should be in a position to respond with greater flexibility to the following conditions:

regional characteristics of the catchment area;

interests, inclinations and aptitudes of different groups of pupils;

the possibility of establishing very close links between the child's familiar environment and what is learnt at school;

the possibility of calling on people from outside the school to cover certain educational material;

the possibility of using the pupil's own environment as a place for learning;

the possibility of using current events in the social environment, reacting to them and reinforcing their impact;

the possibility of creating optimum learning conditions (duration, site, number of people involved, equipment used, etc) and making the most of them;

the possibility of planning and arranging in-service training of teachers geared to the specific needs of their schools.

If the school sets out to act as described above, it will have to be a place where certain educational and training objectives can be satisfactorily achieved and at the same time one which provides all groups concerned with more human living, learning and working conditions.

Evaluation principles
The evaluation of the Tyrolean model of the 'Landhauptschule' (a school in a rural area attended by children between the ages of 10 and 14) observes, as

the description of the project implies, the formative principle whereby data and elements of experience collected on a continuous basis are used to trigger off a retroactive effect in the evaluation team whilst at the same time providing teachers with information on the effects of their individual work performed within the school, and also on what is happening in terms of the project as a whole. This constant communication flow between evaluation/support team and teachers working in schools enables the measures applied to be constantly adjusted and the hypothesis formulated in the project description to be verified whilst ensuring the effective achievement of the objective assigned to the project as a whole.

As regards the preparation of syllabuses for applied and natural sciences, the in-built verification envisaged by the evaluation team consists in guaranteeing and checking that the objectives defined in the syllabus are effectively achieved and that the teaching material prepared for the course is usable (implementation). For experimental work concerning innovative teaching and learning activities (projects, learning to work in a group), the aim of the evaluation is primarily to identify motives (often hidden) underlying the activity which help or hinder the various forms of teaching. As the measures adopted in experimental work are situated at various levels, the evaluation operation selects from among the various possible methods and logical approaches those which can detect effects at the very basis of the experiment, and therefore as close as possible to the 'beneficiaries'. These methods comprise both quantitative data - and feature-collecting processes and qualitative ones (replies from open interviews, analyses of reports of personal experiences, analyses of results, effects of lesson observation etc).

Measures

In the context of evaluation, methods are used which, at a higher level, enable the data collected to be adjusted to provide an objective picture.

So far, the following measures have been adopted in connection with experimental work:

>written reports by the teachers, heads and inspectors concerned, written at the beginning and end of an experimental year, covering attitudes and concrete experiences in relation to certain elements of the experiment;

>collection of statistical data on the measures taken in different schools as part of the experiment, and their consequences (organisation of courses and projects, pupils' participation rates, fluctuation in pupil numbers, courses offered in the pupils' districts of origin, timetables and the number of hours per week allocated to different subjects, amount of travel costs incurred as a result of extra courses, etc);

study of documents prepared in class, particularly in sectors in which new forms of teaching and learning are put to the test;

reports and information on the experiences and observations collected by the support group monitoring the experiment.

Experiences resulting from the experiment were found as follows:
Experiences rated positively:

the reduction in hours is considered by all those involved as an effective means of combating pupil strain and does not cause any drop in performance;

pupils (and parents) act much more responsibly than expected with regard to the optional courses;

the form adopted for initial grading is judged positively by the great majority of teachers concerned;

in-service training for teachers geared to the specific needs of their schools has proved its worth;

the model offers greater latitude for so-called internal school reform (extra programmes for specially gifted children, new forms of learning, etc).

Experiences rated negatively:

teachers and heads have more organisational work to do;

some teachers cannot cope with the complexity of the model;

teachers are worried about unrealistic expectations and inadequate presentations which have been made to the public;

the 'co-management' of school innovations by teachers is very limited;

team-teaching poses great problems for some teachers;

artistic and sports activities are over-represented in the optional course programmes.

Experiences rated positively by some, negatively by others:
> many measures can only be taken on a basis of trust (without prior rules), as verification is not conceivable until afterwards;

> the experiment requires considerable flexibility on the part of the supervisory authorities and school administrations.

COURSE PROTOTYPE TICKET TO BRITAIN

For the past 30 years or so, modern language teaching has been undergoing a dynamic and apparently positive development. At the outset, the teaching of English in schools followed more or less the same pattern as the teaching of classical languages. The emphasis was mainly on learning vocabulary and grammatical rules and translation of English texts into the pupil's own language, ie the *version*. Subsequently, it has been generally agreed that it is not important for the child to be able to recite words or grammatical rules or to produce translations, but to be able to communicate in the language being studied. That is why efforts are currently being made in schools attended by children between the ages of 10 and 14 years (lower secondary schools) to help them acquire the four linguistic skills of speech, comprehension of speech, writing and reading. It is considered self-evident that teaching should take place - to the extent that it is possible and helpful - in English. There is no need for scientific evaluation to demonstrate that pupils learn to communicate much better in the foreign language they study now, than at the time when grammar exercises and translation prevailed.

It is nevertheless a fact that this development in foreign language teaching did not follow a constant progression but rather a zigzag movement: from time to time educational trends gained international prestige and, although they advocated a wide variety of ideas of limited significance, they sought to impose them as universal methods: for instance, the language laboratory method with its 'pattern drill' centred systematically on the learning of structures (see for example, Rivers 1981, page 94 ff), or the radical elimination of any express presentation of grammatical structures to allow 'sub-conscious' language learning, imitating the way children learn their mother tongue (Krashin and Terrell, 1983).

Educational practice, which naturally adopts innovations in teaching methods with some hesitation, has followed a more or less rectilinear course: various innovations have apparently been successfully integrated into teaching as elements of method with a just appreciation of their relative import.

At the present time, research into modern language teaching is being stimulated by a number of factors:

> the growing importance of international exchanges in all fields for which knowledge of a foreign language is indispensable;
>
> the need to offer even the least gifted pupils, for whom the old style curricula did not envisage the teaching of a foreign language, a form of language teaching which will be of practical use to them;
>
> finally, the general educational trend which attaches growing importance to active methods and communicative learning.

The prototype course *Ticket to Britain* tries to go a few steps further in the direction practical language teaching has taken. It sets out in particular:

> to direct the aims and methods of English teaching in upper primary/ lower secondary schools towards greater openness to life and communication situations, and
>
> to adapt the teaching better to the learning capacities and needs of less able pupils attending the 'Hauptschule' (upper primary school), for whom English was introduced into the curriculum as a compulsory subject for the first time in the school year 1986-87.

The evaluation set out below is a comparative study of results obtained by groups of pupils, some of whom were taught on the basis of *Ticket to Britain* and others on the basis of *Ann and Pat*, an English text book which has been in common use in schools for many years. Among other things, this study sets out to establish:

- whether and to what extent less gifted pupils benefit from increased support provided by this new type of teaching;

> what effects teaching based on *Ticket to Britain* has on the results of more able pupils, and
>
> what emotional reaction pupils have to this type of English teaching.

In view of the great complexity of the phenomena to be investigated and the inevitable limits of the experimental framework, the results of this study cannot supply all the information required for a final and irrefutable verdict. Nevertheless, they provide essential elements towards a response to highly divergent expectations, broaden the basis for discussion of teaching methods and contain suggestions likely to stimulate subsequent developments in educational practice.

The two language courses have since been revised, so the comparisons reported will not apply to the versions currently in use. But the main aim of our study was not to compare concrete teaching material but rather to use the experimental method in order to:

> compile elements of information on the effects of different approaches to language teaching, and

> explore methods of systematic evaluation of teaching materials used in language learning.

SUMMARY AND DISCUSSION OF RESULTS
The two language courses:
The experimental course *Ticket to Britain* and the textbook *Ann and Pat* respect the essential principles of modern foreign language teaching: their purpose is not to make the pupil assimilate isolated elements of grammar vocabulary or to stimulate linguistic activity through translation. Both of them set out to give pupils the ability to use the language for communicative purposes and, as a rule, present grammatical structures and vocabulary in a context designed to facilitate their application. In spite of these common features, there are very clear methodological differences between the two courses, at least in the versions on which our study is based.

Ticket to Britain was developed in the framework of a project based on two major objectives: the preparation of teaching materials designed to achieve communication-related objectives in the classroom and to cater for the particular needs of less able pupils. In line with these objectives, efforts are made to give the pupil communicative competences through an intensive study of functional linguistic resources adapted to a set of situations systematically selected for their importance and general scope. Emphasis is primarily based on assimilation of dialogue models, supported in most cases by adaptable 'construction plans'.

In comparison with the official course in use at the time of the experiment, the *Ticket to Britain* course places less emphasis on grammar. The idea behind this is to enable the pupils to acquire a limited number of frequently-used structures in order that they should feel at ease and enjoy communicating. To make the reading texts 'digestible', they are fairly short or sub-divided into small paragraphs and often presented in strip cartoon form.

The course *Ann and Pat* involves a much more pronounced differentiation in teaching; it is organised into three levels from the first class (of lower secondary school) onwards. The course intended for the level I group includes twice as many lexical items and lines of text for reading than that for level III as well as a much greater number of exercises for the study of grammatical structures. Grammar exercises form one of the main elements in the *Ann and Pat* course. Many of these exercises are made up of seven or so questions relating to a clearly defined structural schema. Transformation exercises - transposition of the text from the first person singular to the third or from the present to the past - are not unusual. To help them work on oral expression, pupils are often invited to reply to questions referring to the texts read and/or designed to help them to gain better mastery of certain grammatical structures. They may also be invited to play out dialogues they have read in the textbook.

Effects of the courses on pupil performance:
The results obtained by pupils of the same ability in levels I and II are almost always better in the *Ticket to Britain* than in the *Ann and Pat* course. At level I, the *Ticket to Britain* pupils obtain more or less the same results as the *Ann and Pat* pupils - with the exception of the BIL (picture description) test, in which the *Ann and Pat* pupils performed markedly better. The results of the performance comparison can probably be explained by the following reasons.

The *Ticket to Britain* course enables pupils to acquire complex linguistic resources in a ready-to-use form and applicable to specific situations. Less able pupils find it easier at the start to assimilate complete turns of phrase than to combine previously acquired structures and lexical elements to arrive at the utterance required by the situation. A teaching method of this type does not necessarily present any particular advantage for more gifted children, as they are probably capable of understanding and remembering the grammatical structures and using them as required with a degree of fluency that increases with practice. Conscious and systematic assimilation of grammatical structures might well be a fundamental element essential to the progressive development of their ability to express themselves freely and flexibly in the language studied by automatic combination of its structural and lexical elements.

If this line of reasoning is correct, it will also explain the fact that it is the BIL (picture description) test in which level 1 *Ann and Pat* pupils obtain better results than *Ticket to Britain* pupils of the same ability. In the description of pictures, the *Ticket to Britain* pupil will rarely have the opportunity to apply the ready-made turns of phrase appropriate to particular situations already learned; this pupil will therefore be obliged to construct the appropriate

phrases autonomously by drawing on his structural and lexical knowledge.
To go into more detail, it should be pointed out that:

spelling knowledge is approximately the same for the pupils of the two courses, and

in the *Ticket to Britain* course - in which the texts are fairly short or divided into short passages and abundantly illustrated - less able children achieve somewhat better reading performances.

Sex also plays a much greater role in the differences observed between the pupils than does the textbook used: on average, girls perform notably better in most areas of learning than boys of the same ability, and the superiority of their performance is particularly marked in tasks requiring the production of utterances (picture description test) or words (vocabulary test).

Effects on pupils' motivation, attitudes and feelings
On the whole, no difference was observed between *Ticket to Britain* and *Ann and Pat* pupils at the end of the second year of lower secondary school as regards their opinion on the importance and difficulty of English lessons, anxiety or well-being they experience in class, pleasure in learning, appreciation of the subject and the teacher and assessment of the latter's severity.

However, very clear differences appear when an analysis is carried out on the two groups of pupils by level:

at the (top) level I, the *Ticket to Britain* pupils find the English course easier than do the *Ann and Pat* pupils. They also state that they are less anxious in class;

for the (bottom) level III, the reverse is the case: those following *Ticket to Britain* more frequently state that they find the course difficult and experience more anxiety than the *Ann and Pat* pupils.

To the reader interested in situating the results presented in the context of the historical development and current state of research on language teaching and language learning, we recommend the following works which cover the subject very well: Rivers (1981), Littlewood (1984), Stern (1983) and Kelly (1969).

PILOT RUN OF *LEARNING TO WORK IN A GROUP* COURSES
Introduction

The pilot run of *Learning to Work in a Group* was launched at the start of the school year 1984-85 in a number of general secondary schools in Vienna on the basis of a teacher initiative inspired by the seventh School Organisation Amendment Act. The main aim of this experiment is to help all those involved in schools and teaching, particularly pupils and teachers, to understand one another better. It is hoped to bring about improvements in relations both within these groups and between them.

First of all, it is hoped that a positive influence can be brought to bear on the atmosphere in schools. However, that is not all: the experiment also sets out to trigger off learning processes in pupils which will enable them to acquire an open, prejudice-free attitude towards themselves and their human environment and to act accordingly.

The intention of the programme is that the central aim of learning to work in group courses should be achieved through more concrete goals, towards which specific efforts are directed. Among these goals are:

the development of understanding characterised by respect for others and based on a clear perception of oneself and others;

the establishment of a relationship of trust between pupils and teachers so that they can treat each other as partners while respecting the discipline necessary to the accomplishment of the educational curriculum;

exercise of the ability to co-operate, resolve conflicts, assert oneself and behave autonomously and responsibly in various social situations associated with learning (such as work in a group, with a partner, within a much larger project).

The *Learning to Work in a Group* project attempts to bring school practice closer to a number of great ideals proclaimed so often and so loudly without any effect. The development of courses in this area requires close cooperation between practising teachers and researchers in order to integrate and thereby make the most of the abilities on both sides.

The evaluation of the experiment has the following main objectives:
1 Support of the development work by passing on of intermediate results and scientific advice;
2 Investigation of possibilities and difficulties involved in translating the results obtained within the framework of the project into everyday classroom practice;

3   Final determination of:
   the degree to which the project's objectives are achieved by the methods used and

   positive or negative side-effects observed during the experiment.

Discussion of the results of the study
A provisional overall assessment of the effects of the measures tested within the framework of the *Learning to Work in a Group* experiment brings to light the following elements:

Survey among Teachers

Teachers identify largely with the objectives of the project. The great majority of them take a positive view of the methods applied in the experiment;

Teachers mention as a positive experience a perceptible improvement in contacts and more intensive cooperation with their colleagues;

They consider that these measures make them more inclined to listen to pupils, their problems and interests. They report that pupils have more opportunities to organise their own activities and that those who need help receive it from their classmates more often;

Teachers also mention difficulties, associated in particular with:
- maintaining the necessary discipline;

- limits to the pupils' ability to plan ancarry out their learning activities effectively and responsibly;

- the effort and considerable number of hours required for participation in the experiment.

Survey among Pupils

The pupils in experimental classes judged their teachers' conduct much more favourably than those of control classes. A greater proportion say that teachers take an understanding and sympathetic interest in their personal problems rather than adopting a distant attitude with the primary aim of maintaining discipline (significant correlation 0.25);

A number of indications suggest greater cohesion in the experimental classes than in the control classes;

A tendency was also observed among experimental class pupils to be more motivated by interest in the subject than in the desire to obtain good marks;

Pupils' anxiety, their own estimation of their abilities and their enjoyment of school do not change much following the adoption of measures in the context of the experiment.

The effects of the experimental measures on teachers' objective behaviour are probably much greater than the weak correlations of 0.25, reflecting teacher behaviour as perceived by the pupils, suggest; perception of teacher behaviour is conditioned for the most part by subjective factors within the child's personality.

Non-controlled factors, unanswered questions
In order to be able to make a pertinent judgment on the significance of the results obtained and the evaluation of the experiment, it will be necessary to take into account a number of factors and problems hitherto overlooked.
1. Selection effect - caused by the selection of teachers to participate in the experiment.
2. Hawthorne effect - caused by the more pronounced commitment and time and effort invested to make the project a success, all conditions more favourable than those of day-to-day school practice.
3. Through training of teachers, through regular seminars and meetings.

Should the experiment be continued or not?
The positive results obtained by teachers in the *Learning to Work in a Group* experiment by a conscious and controlled change in their educational practice are very impressive to anyone taking the very limited possibilities of influence into account.
1. Nevertheless it is very probable that the school situation as such has much stronger and more powerful effects on the child than is acknowledged by the educational optimism which seeks to produce large-scale effects by means of ad hoc changes.

2. Another limiting factor is time. If the effect of school on the pupils' personality is limited and the teachers' pedagogical influence only accounts for part of that effect, this will be all the more true of a change in the educational aspects of the school environment limited to a period of one or two years as is the case with the experiment described above.
3. However, another point of view is worth putting forward to avoid underestimation of the significance of the results: whatever its measurable effects on the personalities of pupils and teachers, the creation of an environment which enables all the groups concerned to work in a positive, encouraging and helpful atmosphere may be considered an end in itself. This is true both for teachers (cooperation, job satisfaction) and for pupils (learning environment, school atmosphere). From this particular point of view, the experiment has provided positive and entirely convincing results.

References

KRASHEN, Stephen D. *and* TERRELL, Tracy D. (1983) *The Natural Approach - Language Acquisition in the Classroom.* Oxford: Pergamon Press.

LITTLEWOOD, William T. (1984) *Foreign and Second Language Learning: language acquisition research and its implications for the classroom.* Cambridge: Cambridge University Press.

RIVERS, Wilga M. (1981) *Teaching Foreign-Language Skills in Secondary Education.* Chicago and London: University of Chicago Press.

STERN, H. H. (1983) *Fundamental Concepts of Language Teaching.* Oxford: Oxford University Press.

Evaluation of Educational Programmes: State of the Art in the Netherlands

Wijnand Th . J. G. Hoeben
RION, Institute for Educational Research
University of Groningen

INTRODUCTION
The 1980s might very well prove to be a turning-point in educational evaluation in the Netherlands. Its purposes are changing from predominantly illuminative and formative evaluation towards summative evaluation. Its methodology is changing from a descriptive, process-oriented perspective towards a more output-oriented perspective with a concern for the testing of scientific explanations of outcomes. These developments are partly due to disappointing experiences with the actual uses of evaluations during the 1970s.

This paper will illuminate the turning-point by summing up former and present experiences with purposes, methodologies, and actual uses of evaluations. It will conclude with a discussion of future prospects: developments of Dutch educational evaluation seem to be determined by a desire to get the most out of it.

WHY WE HAVE EVALUATIONS
Dutch educational evaluation during the 1970s and early 1980s consisted of curriculum evaluation and evaluation of (national) programmes for educational innovation. Its purposes were mainly illuminative and formative. A desire to provide teachers, curriculum-developers, educational counsellors and

administrators with helpful insights to improve their participation in the programmes and to improve the programmes themselves was the predominant motive for educational evaluation.

One of the main drawbacks of these purposes was the virtual absence of clear criteria for the success of the curricula and innovative programmes. Successes were mostly defined in terms of implementation (process); successes in terms of educational goals and objectives (outcomes) were neglected. As a consequence the demonstration of benefits and improvements was frequently dependent on ideological discussion instead of empirical argument.

The present trend is to place greater emphasis on successes in terms of intended outcomes and less emphasis on successes in terms of intended processes. Such evaluation might be useful for go/no-go decisions (summative evaluation). In as far as processes and outcomes are linked by causal reasoning and by the testing of resultant hypotheses, such evaluation may also be useful to propose alternative processes, thereby improving the programmes (formative evaluation). Wider audiences too, may derive greater benefit from the present trend.

Further mention may be made of a national periodical assessment study in primary education (since 1987). The purpose of this project is to assess learning outcomes of pupils, thereby estimating and comparing over time the quality of education in important subject areas.

HOW WE DO EVALUATIONS

The methodology of evaluation during the 1970s and early 1980s was mainly descriptive and process-oriented. Such methodology is inspired by and in its turn inspires the illuminative and formative purposes of evaluation, especially as successes are defined in terms of intended implementation of processes. Methods used to describe processes were mainly (participant) observation, interviews, document-analyses and questionnaires.

The methodological orientation on processes was reinforced by the emerging implementation perspective in theories of educational change. As a consequence evaluation studies focused frequently on teachers and school principals as informants. Their levels of concern and their levels of use of an innovation became dependent variables or criteria of qualitative (interviews, document-analysis) and quantitative (questionnaires) approaches. The measurement of educational objectives became during the 1970s a negligible part of educational evaluation (there were some exceptions to this trend, as may be demonstrated by the evaluation studies in Creemers and Verloop, 1984).

The testing of hypotheses on relationships between process variables and outcome variables or the testing of predictions of outcomes that were conditional upon characteristics of the process was rarely incorporated into the design of an evaluation study. The project on 'educational and social environment' is an unequivocal exception during this period (Slavenburg, Van Tilborg and De Visser, 1984).

Scientific criticism however did not become silent altogether. In summary this criticism argued that a process-oriented methodology of evaluation research provides too much leeway for vested interests in a programme (either proponents or opponents) to explain away unwelcome findings.

The present trend may be characterised as an agreement among educational evaluators on at least the following elements:

1. Criteria and standards of a programme have to be formulated and are to be measured in terms of intended outcomes;
2. Causal conclusions have to be made possible in terms of confirmation or refutation of a causal hypothesis;
3. Random assignment to treatments is practically impossible in educational evaluation: therefore quasi-experimental or correlational evaluation designs are to be used;
4. Means (object of evaluation) and ends (criteria of evaluation) provide the rationality of causal hypotheses and conclusions; adequate controls for implementation of a programme and for other systematic influences on its intended outcomes may contribute to an empirical demonstration that observed effects are indeed (or indeed not) consequences of the implementation of the programme.

HOW ARE EVALUATIONS ACTUALLY USED?

Dissatisfaction with the actual use of evaluation has frequently been a motive to propose alternative methodologies. Compared with traditional (quasi-) Research into the use of Dutch educational evaluation however proved the pretensions of alternative methodologies to be unfounded. The evaluations of large-scale innovations in primary education, middle schools, and vocational education, were not used at all: crucial decisions on whether to implement or discontinue the programmes were made before relevant information about the programmes was available (for the case of the middle schools, see Scheerens and Creemers, 1988). Curriculum evaluations within a traditional methodology were compared with those with a process-oriented methodology. The actual use of the last evaluations was less compared with the first (Van de Berg and Hoeben, 1984).

the last evaluations was less compared with the first (Van de Berg and Hoeben, 1984).

Actual use of an evaluation seems not to be a function of alternative methodologies of evaluation, but a function of political and organisational context, especially the presence of conflicting values and interests. The actual use of an evaluation seems furthermore to be a function of the possibilities to explain away unwelcome findings.

PROSPECTS FOR THE FUTURE

To get the most out of evaluations the functions mentioned above should not be neglected. In this context an interesting new model for evaluation research was proposed, the so-called betting model (Hofstee, 1985). Discussions inspired by this proposal have at least led to the methodological agreement between educational evaluators on the elements cited above.

New evaluations of large-scale educational innovations in the Netherlands (educational priorities for disadvantaged learners, and a common curriculum for all pupils from 12 to 16 years of age) are designed along these lines of methodological agreement. Conflicting interests in the political and organisational context have agreed on outcome-based criteria and standards of evaluation. The design of these evaluations makes comparisons possible over time and with reference groups, with controls for the implementation of the programmes and for other influences on the outcomes. With curriculum evaluation comparable developments may be seen (Creemers, 1985).

These developments make it much more difficult for decision-makers to explain away unwelcome findings. From a scientific and professional point of view this seems to be the most important concern of the evaluators. To train new evaluators in a professional role the Universities of Groningen and Twente have founded a centre for educational evaluation to provide postgraduate training and to develop guidelines which would help maximise the potential of investments in educational evaluation.

SELECTED BIBLIOGRAPHY (ENGLISH) ON EVALUATION IN THE NETHERLANDS

VAN DE BERG, G. *and* HOEBEN, W. Th. J. G. (1984) The practice of evaluation research and the use of evaluation results, *Studies in Educational Evaluation,* 10, 3, 309-23.
CREEMERS, B. P. M. *and* Verloop, N. (eds) (1984) Educational evaluation in the Netherlands, *Studies in Educational Evaluation,* 10, 3, 211-341.

anniversary. The Hague: Foundation for Educational Research SVO.

HOEBEN, W. Th. J. G. *and* CREEMERS, B. P. M. (1988) Political backgrounds and innovation strategies as influences on middle school implementation, *International Journal of Educational Research,* 12 (forthcoming).

HOFSTEE, W. K B. (1985) A Bettingmodel of evaluation research. In: CREEMERS B. P. M. (ed) *Evaluation Research in Education. Reflections and Studies. Contributions on the occasion of SVO's twentieth anniversary.* The Hague: Foundation for Educational Research SVO.

SCHEERENS, J. (1987) *Enhancing Educational Opportunities for Disadvantaged Learners: a review of Dutch research on compensatory education and educational development policy.* Amsterdam: North Holland Publishing Company.

SCHEERENS, J. *and* CREEMERS, B. P. M. (1988) Developments in middle school education in Western Europe: educational problems in a nutshell, *International Journal of Educational Research,* 12 (forthcoming).

SLAVENBURG, J. H., VAN TILBORG, L. A. J. *and* DE VISSER, L. (1984) A model for the evaluation of the 'Education and Social Environment' project, *Studies in Educational Evaluation,* 10, 3, 299-309.

The views expressed in this paper are those of the author. They do not necessarily reflect the views of the Institute for Educational Research in the Netherlands (SVO) that has nominated the author as delegate to the workshop.

Norwegian Report

Tom Tiller and Ole Briseid
Det Kongelige Kirke-og Undervisningsdepartment, Oslo

Considerable changes have taken place in the Norwegian school system between 1974 and 1988:
1   New Curriculum Guidelines for primary and lower secondary school (age group 7-16) were introduced in 1974. These Guidelines established the general framework and scope of compulsory education in Norway, including subject syllabuses; see evaluation below. The Curriculum Guidelines were revised in 1985.
2   A new law on Upper Secondary Education (grades 10-12) was also passed in 1974, covering both academic and vocational areas of study. In the fourteen years since then, Norway has seen a movement away from schools offering a limited range of courses within one area of study; approximately 70% of schools now offer courses in several areas of study. There has also been a substantial increase in the number of students in upper secondary schools.
3   There has been a relatively clear tendency towards the decentralisation of control in the case of both compulsory education and upper secondary education. More responsibility has been delegated from the national to the regional and local level.
4   Handicapped pupils have been integrated into the regular school system wherever possible.
5   Comparatively large sums of money have been spent on programmes devoted to organisational development and leadership, with a view to improving the administration of schools. See evaluation below.
6   We have in this period seen the rapid development and decentralisation of higher education in the form of regional colleges.
7   Apprenticeship training in industry has also expanded strongly.

We in Norway now recognise that the evaluation of changes and new approaches in the educational system has been unsatisfactory. This led us this year to establish a Centre for Educational Research. One of the Centre's main tasks will be to encourage the development of competence in evaluation research into the educational system. A large programme of research into the administration, organisation and control of the school system has also been initiated, and evaluation research will be a central aspect of the work. The purpose of these moves is partly to make a thorough evaluation of the changes that have taken place during the last fourteen years.

In 1987 the OECD published two surveys of Norway, one of the Norwegian educational system as a whole, and one of the plan for the development of information technology in Norwegian basic and upper secondary schools.

Four large-scale national surveys undertaken in Norway during recent years are outlined.

AN INVESTIGATION INTO THE INTENTIONS OF THE CURRICULUM GUIDELINES

This was a broad evaluative project whose goal was to gain information as to whether and to what extent the aims and intentions of the curriculum guidelines had been realised. The project was carried out in the period 1978-1983.

The work focused on four main areas:
> the schools' use of their resources;
>
> how the teaching was organised;
>
> cooperation within schools;
>
> the factual content of school teaching

Twenty-six reports dealing with specific parts of the project were published. The empirical contributions were based primarily on completed questionnaires and concentrated on the registration of resources. The results were presented more as descriptions of activity in schools than as basic analyses and evaluations.

Two other reports on the fulfilment of the aims of the Curriculum Guidelines had a rather different point of departure. These reports showed clearly that the criteria for the evaluation, in particular the phrase 'intentions of the Curriculum Guidelines', were far from unambiguous within the framework of the unitary Norwegian school.

The Ministry of Education also granted three million kroner to research work in connection with this project. The results of this research were not published in their entirety through the project itself; extracts were presented in a specially compiled report.

Despite its ambitious aims, the project does not seem to have initiated the hoped-for discussions on the place and function of schools, and it is not clear what consequences the work had for day-to-day life in schools.

THE SCHOOL: MILIEU AND LEADERSHIP

'The school: milieu and leadership' was a nationwide project which was carried out in the period 1980-1987 in Norwegian primary and lower secondary schools. The estimated cost of the entire project was approximately sixty million kroner. In addition to the ongoing evaluation, two large-scale assessments were undertaken, commissioned by the National Council for Basic Education. The first, published in 1985, was partly an investigation on the basis of questionnaires, and partly a case study of eleven schools.

The final project assessment was carried out in 1986-1987 by the University of Oslo. The work was threefold:

analysis of project premises;

analysis of the project programme and organisation;

analysis of project execution and associated activities.

In evaluating the programme, the basis of the project was assessed in the light of the authors' analysis of necessary leadership qualities (project premises). While the authors' stated view related leadership qualities to the social environment in which the school is placed, their own *de facto* point of departure was the pedagogical/didactical leader.

The analysis of the execution of the project and its related activities was based on the collection of data through the completion of questionnaires and interviews. In the light of the fact that this was a nationwide project, the empirical basis for conclusions was thin. In view of the authors' conception of leadership qualities, the project, it is concluded, is of limited value with regard to the training of school personnel in leading positions. Both large-scale assessments have been given a partly negative reception by the project leaders and the body which commissioned the project.

ORGANISATIONAL DEVELOPMENT (OD)

OD in the basic school

This project was carried out in three regional authorities in 1974-1984, under the direction of the National Council for Innovation in Education. A total of fifteen schools participated in the whole project. The final project assessment was presented in the form of a relatively brief and concise summary which aimed at shedding light on the following questions:

1 Has the project followed the anticipated strategy? What has changed, and how can this be explained?
2 What conditions must be met for the project plan to work?

3   What conditions, in our experience, must be met before development work in a specific school takes place?

The assessment was undertaken by representatives of the project group and the National Council for Innovation in Education. It must therefore be looked upon as an internal assessment. The empirical material was collected by means of questionnaires, ongoing reports from schools/project groups, and interviews. Material based on the questionnaires is dominant in the assessment as presented. Particularly in the light of the complexity that seems to characterise OD in an educational context (cf Fullan, Miles & Taylor, 1980), it must be admitted that this assessment offers a somewhat superficial analysis of important questions. It will only to a limited extent fulfil its own aim of 'broadening our *understanding* of what OD in schools presupposes, implies and results in'.

OD in the upper secondary school
The National Council for Upper Secondary Education has introduced OD in several regions of Norway in the period since 1979. The project includes the training of OD advisers and the carrying out of concrete OD projects in schools. Up to the present, the projects have been subject to *internal* assessment by one of those mainly responsible. In addition, an *external* evaluation is in progress, under the aegis of the University of Tromsø. No large final report has resulted from the internal assessment. From the external evaluation, two reports have so far been published. It is now nearing completion.

   In addition to continuous course assessment, the internal assessment has primarily provided empirical data through completed questionnaires. The external evaluation, covering the four most northerly regions in Norway, has a broad methodical approach. Questionnaires, interviews, course reports, case studies, reports from participants, diaries kept by OD advisers and official publications are all made use of. The views of all those who form the social entity that we call school are regarded as important. The objectives of the external evaluation are largely in line with the questions mentioned in connection with the OD project in the Basic School.

References
FULLAN, M., MILES, M. *and* TAYLOR, G. (1980) Organisation development in schools: the state of the art, *Review of Educational Research*, 50.1.

Spanish Experience With Evaluation in the Educational Field

Mariano Alvaro Page
Director of the Assessment Service of CIDE, Madrid

There is currently a sharp awareness in Spain on the need to have updated data available on the performance of the educational system. This necessarily leads to an evaluation process boom heightened by efforts under way to introduce in-depth changes at the different levels of the Spanish educational system.

From that we may infer that the attraction of educational evaluation lies in the fact that it helps to find out the state of the issue, to implement the relevant changes and to check whether such implementation has been in accordance with the objectives set out in advance.

There are several bodies in Spain concerned with educational evaluation as one of their basic activities, particularly the Centro de Investigación y Documentación Educativa, which has a specific Evaluation Service, and the Technical Inspection Service which focuses on Primary (General Basic Education) and Secondary Education levels. Both report to the Ministry of Education and Science.

We summarise below the most significant evaluation projects carried out in the Spanish context.

EXTERNAL EVALUATION OF SECONDARY EDUCATION REFORM

The main purpose of this project is to examine whether the new curriculum would lead to better, similar or poorer results than those achieved through the educational system in force (Vocational Training and Unified and Polyvalent Baccalaureate). The Reform or experimental education was initiated in a bid to mitigate the huge differences between these two forms of education, between which students had to choose at the age of 14.

The study covers two generations of students. One entered secondary education in 1984 and the other in 1985. Within each of these generations, three groups have been selected: the *experimental* group (about 3,400 students in experimental education), the *internal control* group (about 2,500 students taking the normal curriculum at experimental centres) and the *external control* group (about 8,300 students taking the normal curriculum at non-experimental centres).

Each generation takes part in several assessments (pretest and one or two post-tests). Various tests are applied to each of them to evaluate the *skills, attitudes and achievement* of the students over a period of two years.

Achievement is measured through objective tests and through school marks. The objective tests evaluate the general objectives of the secondary education curriculum and the basic knowledge and skills in Primary Education instrumental subjects (language and maths).

The abilities evaluated have been: verbal, numerical, logical reasoning, mechanical and spatial abilities.

Civic-social attitudes, emotional reactions towards studying, expectations and didactical aspects have also been measured.

All the assessment instruments have been completed and *final reports* have been drawn up on one of the generations evaluated.

The results of this study show that there are two subcultures: Unified and Polyvalent Baccalaureate and Vocational Training; VT students show a lower level of achievement, a lower level of skills, a lower level of academic-professional expectations, less democratic civic-social attitudes and less positive feelings towards studying. However, when students in experimental education are considered, they are found to attain similar achievements to their Unified and Polyvalent Baccalaureate counterparts and, additionally, their academic performance is clearly better than that of VT students.

Summing up, we may conclude that the Reform substantially improves the performance of the 'poorer' students while hardly lowering that of the 'better' ones.

The centre responsible for this evaluation is the Centro de Investigación y Documentación Educativa.

INTERNATIONAL EVALUATION PROJECT

Spain is taking part, along with Canada, Korea, Great Britain, Ireland and the United States, in an international project coordinated by the Educational Testing Service (ETS), whose purpose is to evaluate the achievement of 13-year-old students in the areas of Science and Mathematics.

The sample in each country is made up of 20 students chosen at each of 100 centres, so that the final sample per country is 2,000 students.

The tests to be applied are as follows:
- Maths test;
- Science Test;
- Student questionnaire;
- Teacher questionnaire on 'opportunity to learn'.

These tests were drawn up on the basis of the item 'pool' held by the ETS for the National Assessment of Educational Progress.

Following an initial meeting, curriculum experts from the different countries taking part in the project selected the items which suited the curriculum of each country. Then a second meeting was held between these experts in order to select the items which were common to every country. These common items were tested through pilot studies. As a result of these pilot studies, the items which were to be included in the final tests were chosen.

The test administration was carried out in February 1988, and the representatives of the countries taking part in the project are scheduled to meet in September of this year to draw up the final report.

The body responsible for carrying out this empirical work on the part of Spain is the Centro de Investigación y Documentación Educativa.

EVALUATING THE REFORM OF THE UPPER PRIMARY EDUCATION CYCLE

In general, the aim is to understand the general process of education in a specific context arising from curricular renewal, taking into account how the basic ideas of the renewal project are *assumed* by all those concerned, how the practice *changes* and how these changes can be reflected in various *learning results*.

The main groups of variables under review, or the most relevant features of the process of implementing a new curriculum, are as follows:

> The *context* of the curricular reform. Initial diagnosis. Concerns the situation to be altered through the proposed reform;
>
> *Curriculum.* Intrinsic evaluation of the proposed curriculum;
>
> *Strategy for innovation.* Strategy for implementing the reform and channels as well as tools to be used in disseminating it.

Process of implementing the reform. Process reviewed at three levels:
- Preactive dimension of education. How teachers translate the principles of the reform drawing up their own curricular plan;
- Interactive dimension. The practice of education at the centres undergoing reform;
- Evaluation of the curriculum by the teachers. Knowledge and skills which teachers take into account in monitoring achievement.

The research report is made up of five parts:
   The reform students;
   The reform teachers;
   The centres taking part in the reform;
   The teaching-learning process in the reform;
   The parents in the face of reform.

The centre responsible for the project is the Centro de Investigación y Documentación Educativa.

REPORT ON EVALUATION OF THE MINIMUM TO BE TAUGHT IN THE INITIAL AND MIDDLE PRIMARY EDUCATION CYCLES.

In order to find out the educational results of Primary Education, the Ministry of Education and Science carried out an evaluation of the Initial Cycle in 1983 and an evaluation of the Middle Cycle in 1985.

The subject of the evaluation was the *minimumto be taught* in both cycles because, firstly, this includes not only the knowledge to be acquired but also the skills to be developed and the attitudes to be incorporated, and, secondly, because of its general nature, as the *minimum to be taught* affects the whole of the domestic territory.

The tools were drawn up by teams from the Ministry of Education and Science and the Regional Governments which have full powers concerning educational matters, under the coordination of a Primary Education Inspector.

In drawing up these tools, the *minimum to be taught* was specified in the form of educational objectives, in order to make a selection of these. On the basis of the objectives, certain items were drawn up and, in turn, a selection of these was used in drawing up the questionnaires. A team of experts also drew up questionnaires for teachers, parents and students.

The sampling was taken at random, using a stratified procedure with proportional affixation, on the basis of the legal system, the structure and location of the centres.

The results were analysed and interpreted at the Directorate General of Primary Education, by the School Evaluation Service.

A report was drawn up in 1984 on 'Evaluation of the Minimum to be Taught in the Initial Cycle of Primary Education', which was published by the Ministry of Education and Science. The report concerning the Middle Cycle has already been published, but is at the stage of determining how it should be distributed.

Both reports, besides all that concerns the processing, presentation and analysis of the results, include the evaluation tools which have been used.

DRAWING UP TOOLS FOR EVALUATING BASIC ASPECTS OF STUDENT ACHIEVEMENT IN THE 8TH GRADE OF PRIMARY EDUCATION

The objective of the project is to draw up tools for evaluating the abilities and skills which students have acquired on the basis of their respective aptitudes and of the content of and activities carried out in their school work.

These tools could allow:

(a) Centres to obtain sufficient data for finding out their position at the national, regional, provincial or local level and take any measures which may be appropriate;

(b) Students and teachers to evaluate themselves in the aspects considered;

(c) The Administration to compare the achievement of centres at different times, and propose corrective measures.

The variables considered in selecting the sample were: sex, system and type of centre. The sampling was taken in eight provinces.

The tests drawn up for the purpose concern Language, Maths, and Attitudes towards studying and intellectual work techniques.

The centre responsible for this work is the Directorate General of Coordination and Senior Inspection.

EVALUATION OF THE FINAL LEVELS IN THE DIFFERENT FORMS OF SECONDARY SCHOOLING

The primary objective of this research project is to evaluate a series of educational aspects - skills, knowledge, attitudes, etc. - of 18-year-old students who in the 1988-89 school year are in the final levels of the different forms of secondary schooling currently available - Course of University Orientation, 2nd course of Second Grade Vocational Training, and 2nd cycle of the Secondary Schooling Reform.

This empirical work under way will allow an assessment to be made of students completing their secondary schooling, as well as to evaluate students who are in the second cycle of the experimental plan and, finally, to compare the results obtained in the three types of education.

Finally, the Education Technical Inspection Service draws up annual reports on the performance of the initial-cycle Primary Education units and of Secondary Education centres.

Selective Bibliography Prepared by the Scottish Council For Research in Education

Introduction

The purpose of the workshop is to provide a forum for debate between those who carry out evaluations and those who use them. This bibliography has been prepared as an informal background document for delegates to aid interpretation and understanding of the methodological background to the evaluations discussed.

The items cited derive from two sources: (a) a small number of individuals in the United Kingdom with experience of evaluations and (b) participants at a recent meeting of the Colloquy of Directors of Educational Research Institutions. Each was asked to supply 'bibliographical references to the five recent pieces of writing which are seen, in your country, to be the most important in relation to methodology and approaches to the evaluation of educational programmes. The works cited may be 'practical' as well as theoretic and need not necessarily be published within your country'. This document brings together the responses to this request.

The organisers are most grateful to all those who submitted information, and in particular to those who went to considerable trouble to provide contextualised background notes.

Bibliography

BELGIUM

Respondent's comment:

A short introduction might help to clarify the answer to your question: in general, Belgian researchers don't feel the need to produce original theoretical publications on methodology and approaches to the evaluation of educational programmes. It is not their primary goal. Influenced by what goes on in OECD-meetings, AERA-conferences, IEA-meetings, UNESCO-meetings etc, they usually find their basic methodological framework in the Anglo-Saxon literature. From then on evaluation projects are developed and implemented on a cooperative (eg IEA) or an individual base.

On the other hand, however, the expertise of Belgian senior researchers on methodological problems is often demanded by international organisations like UNESCO.

All the important evaluation projects in education are published in the R & D-Bulletins - of the Council of Europe. Analyses of the contents of these projects can provide an overview of the main topics we are actually interested in. Since the last decennium, Belgium universities are more and more involved in evaluation projects which are responsive to the specific needs and demands of educational policy-makers.

Now comes the specific answer to your question: rather than start with the name of the authors I prefer to specify the domains in which they are active.

(1) Quantitative research: MACRO EVALUATION

The studies of the International Association for the Evaluation of Educational Achievement (IEA).

Since 1968 Belgium has contributed actively in these projects:
(International volumes: see Appendix 1, page 12)
in press: - The International Mathematics Curriculum
- Cross-sectional Report
- Longitudinal Report

Belgian senior researchers:
- French-speaking Belgium (University of Liège): G. Henry
- Flemish-speaking Belgium (University of Ghent): C. Brusselmans-Dehairs.

(2) Qualitative research: theoretical consideration and evaluation of school innovation processes.

VANDENBERGHE, R. *and* VANDENBERG, R. (1981) *Onderwijsinnovatie in Verschuivend Perspectief.* Tilburg.
VANDENBERG, R. *and* VANDENBERGHE, R. (1984) *Grootschaligheid in de Onderwijsvernieuwing.* Meerhout: Infobox.
R. Vandenberg is the Belgian researcher (University of Louvain) who introduced the concept 'School innovations in Belgium'. He is considered the Belgian expert in this field.

DE BLOCK, A. *and* HEENE, J. (1986) *Inleiding tot de algemene didactiek.* Antwerpen: Standaard Educatieve Uitgeverij, 10.
This 10th edition proves that this work has been and still is a bestseller in the Flemish part of the country. It focuses attention on many aspects of the teaching and learning processes and provides a number of opportunities to improve the quality of micro-education.

DE LANDSHEERE, G. (1982) *Introduction à la Recherche en Education.* Liège: Ed. Thone.
DE LANDSHEERE, G. (1986) *La Recherche en Education dans le Monde.* Paris: PUF.
In Belgium, G De Landsheere is considered a pioneer and an expert in the domain of educational sciences. He has contributed very much to the dissemination of American research expertise in our country.

DE CORTE, E. (n.d.) *Learning and Instruction: European research in an international context.* Vol.1. (Chairman of the EARLI-group.)

CYPRUS
BLOOM, B. *et al* (1956) *Taxonomy of Educational Objectives: the classification of educational goals. Handbook 1: Cognitive domain.* New York: D. McKay.
BLOOM, B. *et al* (1971) *Handbook on Formative and Summative Evaluation of Student Learning.* New York: McGraw Hill.
GRONLUND, N.E. (1981) *Measurement and Evaluation in Teaching.* New York: Macmillan Publ. Co. Inc.

HOPKINS, C.D. *and* ANTES, R.L.(1978) *Classroom Measurement and Evaluation.* Ippinois: F.E. Peacock Pub. Inc.

THORNDIKE, R.L. *and* HAGEN, E.P. (1977) *Measurement and Evaluation in Psychology and Education.* New York: John Wiley and Sons.

DENMARK
Respondent's comment:
Having discussed the issue with colleagues here at the institute as well as the University of Copenhagen I arrived at the conclusion that the most important thing to be said is that it will hardly be possible to point out specific references as *the* most important with reference to methodology to Danish researchers within this field of research.

That said, it would be fair to mention that within the last few years there have been strong tendencies in Denmark to supplement or substitute purely quantitative forms of collection of data for evaluation by other forms offering, to a higher degree, possibilities of qualitative analyses. In this connection, I find it difficult to point out 'principal works'.

FEDERAL REPUBLIC OF GERMANY
Respondent's comment:
None of the titles is actually new. This is obviously a result of the fact that research into evaluation has at present no great importance within educational research.

BLANKERTZ, H. (ed) (1986) *Lernen und Kompetenzentwicklungen in der Sekundarstufe II - Abschlussbericht der Wissenschaftlichen Begleitung Kollegstufe Nordrhein-Westfalen zur Evaluation von vier Doppeltqualifizierenden Bildungsgängen des Kollegschulversuches in den Schwerpunkten Fremdsprachen - Physik - Erziehung - Sport.* [Learning and development of competence in secondary II - final report etc.] Soest.

BUND/LANDER KOMMISSION FUR BILDUNGSPLANUNG UND FORSCHUNGSFORDERUNG (ed) (1981) *Dimensionen und Grenzen der Evaluation Schulischer Neuerungen - Bericht uber ein CERI-Seminar.* [Dimensions and limits of evaluation of innovations in schools: report of a CERI seminar.] Stuttgart.

BUND/LANDER KOMMISSION FUR BILDUNGSPLANUNG UND FORSCHUNGSFORDERUNG (ed) (1984) *Evaluation von Modellversuchen - Bericht über die CERI/OECD Seminarreite 1977 bis 1981.* [Evaluation of model experiments: report of a series of CERI/OECD seminars 1977-1981, FDR, Austria, Switzerland.] Bonn.

FEND, Helmut (1982) *Gesamtschule im Vergleich - Bilanz der Ergebnisse des Gesamtschulversuches.* [Comprehensive schools compared: review of the results of the comprehensive school experiment.] Weinheim/Basel.

MITTER, W. *and* WEISHAMPT, H. (eds) (1977) *Ansatze zur Analyse der Wissenschaftlichen Begleitung Bildungspolitischer Innovationen.* [Start for the analysis of the scientific commentary of educational-political innovations.] Weinheim/Basel.

IRELAND

Respondent's comment:

I have identified five titles which I regard as important. The selection is a personal one and I cannot say that it represents the views of people 'in my country'. You will note that all the titles might not meet the criterion 'recent'. I think there has been relatively little development in the field of evaluation in recent years; much recent American literature, for example, is devoted to testing rather than to wider evaluation issues. You will also note that all the titles are American.

COOK, T.D. (1985) Postpostivist critical multiplism. In: SHOTLAND, R.L. and MARK, N. M. (eds). *Social Science and Social Policy.* London: Sage.

JACOB, E. (1988) Clarifying qualitative research. A focus on traditions, *Educational Research,* 7, 1, 16-24.

STUFFLEBEAM, D. L. *and* WEBSTER, W. J. (1988) Evaluation as an administrative function. In: BOYAN, N. J. (ed) *Handbook of Research on Educational Administration.* London: Longman.

UNITED STATES JOINT COMMITTEE ON STANDARDS FOR EDUCATIONAL EVALUATION (1981) *Standards for the Evaluation of Educational Programs, Projects, and Materials.* New York: McGraw-Hill.

WEISS, C. H. (1979) The many meanings of research utilization, *Public Administration Review,* 39, 426-431.

NETHERLANDS

Respondent's comment:
You will find enclosed a list of important recent Dutch publications on the evaluation of educational programmes. As you will see, most texts were originally written in the Dutch language. For your convenience I give a short description in English for each of them.

(1) General methodological topics
DE GROOT, A. D. (1986) *Begrip van Evalueren*. [Knowing Evaluation.] Den Haag.

In the Netherlands A.D. De Groot is seen as one of the important experts in the domain of the methodology of educational research. The present book deals with processes and conditions that are fundamental to good organisation of the evaluation of educational programmes. In the first place he describes the type of problems dealt with in evaluation research. Research questions, methods for data-analysis and the problem-bound type of cooperation between educational practice and research are important themes. An important problem he deals with in his book concerns the evaluation of national educational systems. He points out that such evaluation is in need of a well-defined theory. One of the main problems in the organisation of such evaluation is the lack of commitment/ agreement towards/about the goals of the school system. In an attempt to clarify this discussion De Groot focuses on the student's learning outcomes or learning experiences and how they may be measured. The author stresses the importance of learner- related goals. In his goalmatrix half the goals may be qualified as learner-related. He points out that this type of goal is neglected in the present school system.

De Groot actually values only one type of evaluation, the evaluation done by independent investigators with the aim of knowing the outcomes, the output of a programme. This does not mean that De Groot approaches the evaluated process as if it were a black box. Chapter 6 contains a well-thought-out description of the processes of planning and evaluating educational programmes. Much attention is given to the question of whether a curriculum covers the knowledge domains that are referred to in the definition of educational objectives. In this context process evaluation gets a clear position in a cycle of reasonable/rational goal directed activities.

In the case of the fundamental question as to whether the quality of education may be measured, De Groot's answer is that quality should always be seen as a characteristic of the dependent variable: innovations in education are not automatically improvements. Whether they are improvements is an empirical question that should be investigated. De Groot argues in favour of a problem-directed evaluation strategy. His opinion is that the classical experimental design should stay the norm for evaluations of evaluation activities. At this point he clearly differs from Cronbach.

After De Groot in the art of evaluation methodology, one of the more challenging points is not excluding anything that possibly could be meaningful. Even aspects or processes that characterise the object that should be evaluated, and that which, on first sight seems irrational and irrelevant deserves reflection. Over and over again De Groot points at the risks of narrowing interpretations of methodological rules or principles.

HOFSTEE, W. K. B. (1980) *De Empirische Discussie: theorie van het sociaal wetenschappelijk onderzoek.* [The Empirical Discussion: theory of the research in the social sciences.] Amsterdam.

Actually this book was published rather a long time ago. Recently, however some Dutch evaluation researchers started using the book as a kind of guideline, because it contains a description of the so-called 'model for betting'. With this model Hofstee stresses how important it is that research theories specify criteria for the evaluation of the consistency and reality content of empirical statements. In order to make this feasible Hostee describes as a requirement that the statements are defined as predictions, and that the predicting value can be compared with the predicting value of other statements. With these conditions satisfied criterium descriptions in research practice might be effective if persons or organisations involved in the implementation of the treatment that is the object of the evaluation, respect and accept the research outcomes as the basis for decisions in respect of the question who is right and who is wrong. Together these conditions realise a situation in which a bet functions as a model for empirical discussions. Hofstee presents this model as the result of attempts rigorously to represent empirical (social) science as a social activity. He is convinced that the model may help in cleaning up the litterlike mass which, as he sees it, characterises the social sciences. He thinks that this mass is the consequence of incapacity in defining criteria for the demarcation of empirical statements in a research tradition in which science is approached as a product. Because this tradition is so commonly accepted, investigators actually started to believe that those criteria really cannot be found. Too often researchers act as if they have overcome this self-created crisis by leaving their concept of knowledge undefined, unspecified. Others try to find the solution in sharply defining criteria for demarcation in the context of a notion of empirical science as a interesting point in this investigation is the use of matrix-sampling. Each student completes only a sample from the larger pool of test items.

PORTUGAL
No information available.

SPAIN
ALVARO, M. et al (1988) *Evaluacion Externa de la Reforma del primer cicpo de Ensenanzas Medias (II Generacion)*. Madrid: Ministerio de Educacion y Ciencia.

BEATON, A. E. et al (1987) *The NAEP 1983 - 84 Technical Report*. Princeton: Educational Testing Service.

BOCK, R. D. and MISLEVY, R. J. (1986) *Comprehensive Educational Assessment for the States: the Duplex design*. University of Chicago.

CRONBACH, L. J. (1982) *Designing Evaluations of Educational and Social Programs*. San Francisco: Jossey Bass.

MESSICK, S., BEATON, A. E. and LORD, F. (1983) *A New Design for a New Era*. Princeton: Educational Testing Service.

PATTON, M. Q. (1980) *Qualitative Evaluation Methods*. Sage.

RUTMAN, L. (1984) *Evaluation Research Methods*. Sage.

SANDEFUR, G. D., ROSSI, P. H. and FREEMAN, H. E. (1986) *Workbook for Evaluation*. Sage.

STUFFLEBEAM, D. L. and SHINKFIELD, A. J. (1987) *Evaluacion Sistematica*. Madrid: Ministerio de Education y Ciencia.

SWITZERLAND
CARDINET, J. and WEISS, J. (1978) *L'observation Interactive, au Confluent de la Formation et de la Recherche*. Neuchatel: Institut romand de recherches et de documentation pedagogiques. IRDP/R 78.16

CARDINET, J. (1985) *A la Poursuite de l'objectivite dans l'evaluation des Innovations Pedagogiques*. Neuchatel: Institut romand de recherches et de documentation pedagogiques. IRDP/R 78.16

CARDINET, J. and TOURNEUR, Y. (1985) *Assurer la Mesure: guide pour les etudes de generalisabilite*. Berne: Peter Lang. Collection Exploration, Serie Cours et contributions pour les sciences de l'education.

---

mere procedure.

In his model for betting he avoids the problem of the crisis by introducing rules for deciding on statements, scoring rules as criteria for demarcation and rules for formulating personal predictive distributions of probability.

(2) The evaluation of programmes for compensatory education and for the promotion of family involvement.

SLAVENBURG, J. H. (1986) *Onderwijsstimulering en Gezinsactivering*. [Compensatory Education and Family Involvement.] Den Haag.

VAN TILBORG, I. A. J. (1987) *De Betekenis van het Arbeidersgezin voor het Leerniveau ende Schoolloopbaan van het Kind*. [The Importance of the Working Class Family for the Level of Achievement and the School Career of the Child.] Den Haag.

DE VISSER, L. (1987) *Leerlingkenmerken en Schoolloopbaan van 4-7-jarige Arbeiderskinderen*. [Pupil Characteristics and School Career of 4-7-Year-Olds with a Working Class Family Background.] Den Haag.

These publications are the reports of the evaluation of the first part of the Dutch project Education and Social Environment (OSM).

This project is one out of three innovation projects that SVO started financing in the sixties and seventies. The other two are: the Amsterdam innovation project and the Utrecht project (GEON).

OSM is the broadest and most important compensatory education project in the Netherlands which is subsidised for approximately 20 years. The project develops, evaluates and distributes programmes for children of kindergarten and primary school age from lower S. E. S. -groups.

The compensatory programmes aim at the development of cognitive and emotional pupil characteristics. At the same time it attempted to raise mathematical and language skills and knowledge by means of well-structured programmes.

The family involvement programmes were aimed at stimulating parents to support their children's school careers.

The project's development task finished in 1986. The evaluation programme started in 1978 and will finish in 1989. This programme's goal is to find out to what extent the programmes were adopted in schools and families and what short term effects they have and in what sense and to what extent these effects may be called transfer effects.

In relation to this evaluation a study has been set up which explores what variables affect the school achievements of pupils with a lower SES-background and to what extent the effects of these variables may be influenced.

As stated before, these publications cover the first part of the evaluation programme (4-8 year-olds).

BEEM, A. L. (ed) (1988) *Weten, Redeneren, Raden* [Knowing, Reasoning, Guessing.] Lisse.

The Dutch Government recently decided to introduce a basic, comprehensive curriculum for all 12-15 year-olds in the Netherlands. This curriculum is aimed at:

- raising the level of education for youth;
- the broadening and deepening of the common cultural basis;
- (adaption to) requirements which are imposed by technological and socio-cultural developments;
- lessening the inequality of opportunities by avoiding an early irreversible choice for study or a profession.

A nationwide evaluation project that starts in 1988 and finishes in 1999 should give information about the extent to which the goals are attained and about the ways in which schools realise the basic common curriculum.

An analytical evaluation was set up with the aim of generating questions that may be evaluated in the context of this policy-programme and in order to be able to plan the evaluation.

This analytical evaluation clearly is an experiment. Never before in the Netherlands have investigators explored in such a well-planned manner the consequences that particular policies may have for the evaluation of policy.

Experts from the domain of educational psychology, curriculum/didactics and the sociology of education were asked to study particular aspects of the policy in relation to the evaluation. This has resulted in proposals for evaluation studies which are rather well specified.

It is remarkable is that there was so much agreement between the experts about the order of different steps in the evaluation research, about the supposed effects, and about the way the research has to be structured/ organised. Moreover, some proposals stress the importance of an active self-evaluation by schools with the goal of improving the efficacy and output of the innovation.

KLOPROGGE, J. J. J. (1987) *Uitvoeringsplan Evaluatie Onderv Voorrangsbeleid 1989 - 1990.* [Programme for the evaluation of policy towards educational preference areas.] Den Haag.

In 1987 a nationwide evaluation programme was started in relation to a government policy towards the improvement of educational and professi opportunities for minority students (students with a non-Dutch cul background and Dutch students with a lower SES-background).

This policy is characterised by two types of measures.

The first concerns the organisation of cooperation between schoo welfare organisations in particluar local regions. Together they shoul towards an activity plan aimed at improving the cognitive and em development of primary school children and the children in the first y secondary schools.

The second consists of funding extra teachers for schools.

An important difference between this project and for example th project which was referred to before, is that the evaluation program more complex. In the OSM-project the contents and goals of the in were the same for all participating schools. The programme for the the educational preference areas is a programme which offers variety of means for achieving the goals. Schools may choose differ which satisfy their specific needs.

The evaluation programme deals with the premises for evaluati attention is given to the research design, and to the implications policy-making. The publication concludes with an overview of evaluation process.

WIJNSTRA, J. M. (1987). *Periodieke Peiling van het Onde Meerjarenplan 1988 - 1991 en Werkplan 1988.* [The Recurren of the Level of Education. A programme for 1988-1991 and plan for 1988.] Arnhem.

Nationwide recurrent assessment of the level of education wa the aim of measuring the quality of the curriculum in primar measuring students' learning achievements. In a national sam students take tests in arithmetic, Dutch language, traffic educati social studies, gymnastics, health education and in English. was started in 1987 and should be ready by the end of 1990.

Each year, students take a test halfway through the schoo at the end of the school year, for two content domains. questionnaires on the curriculum content taught. A r

PERRET, J. F. (1985) *Comprendre l'ecriture des Nombres.* These de doctorate, Berne: Peter Lang. Collection Exploration, Serie Recherche en sciences de l'education.

PERET, J. F. (1988) *IRDP, Connaissances Mathematiques a l'ecole Primaire: presentation et synthese d'une evaluation romande.* Fascicule introductif. Berne; Peter Lang. Collection Exploration, Serie Cours et contributions pour les sciences de l'education.

HUBERMAN, M. *and* MILES, M. (1983) *L'analyse des Donnees Qualitatives: quelques techniques de reduction et de representation.* Neuchatel: Institut romande de recherches et de documentation pedagogiques. IRDP/R 83.03. Collection Cahier du GCR/SSRE No.6

UNITED KINGDOM

This list includes 'classics' as well as more recent publications. Where titles are known to be out of print this has been noted.

ADELMAN, C. *and* ALEXANDER, R. J. (1982) *The Self-Evaluating Institution.* London: Methuen.

ADELMAN, C. (ed) (1984) *The Politics and Ethics of Evaluation.* London: Croom Helm.

CRONBACH, L. J. (1980) *Towards Reform of Program Evaluation.* San Francisco: Jossey Bass.

EISNER, E. W. (1979) *The Educational Imagination: on the design and evaluation of school programs.* New York: Macmillan.

GUBA, E. G. *and* LINCOLN, Y. S. (1981) *Effective Evaluation: improving the usefulness of evaluation results through responsive and naturalistic approaches.* San Francisco: Jossey Bass.

HAMILTON, D. *et al* (1977) *Beyond the Numbers Game.* London: Macmillan. (Out of Print.)

HARLEN, W. (ed) (1979) *Evaluation and the Teacher's Role.* London: Macmillan.

HOUSE, E. R. (1980) *Evaluating with Validity.* Beverley Hills: Sage.

MCCORMICK, R. *and* JAMES, M. (1983) *Curriculum Evaluation in Schools.* London and Canberra: Croom Helm.

MURPHY, R. *and* TORRANCE, Harry (eds) (1987) *Evaluating Education: issues and methods - an Open University reader.* London: Harper and Row.

SCRIVEN, M. (1973) *Goal-Free Evaluation.* Berkeley: McCutchan.

SHIPMAN, M. (1979) *In-School Evaluation.* London: Heineman. (Out of print).
SIMONS, H. (1987) *Getting to Know Schools in a Democracy: the politics and process of evaluation.* Lewes: Falmer Press.
SKILBECK, M. (ed) (1984) *Evaluating the Curriculum in the Eighties.* London: Hodder and Stoughton.
STAKE, R. (1976) *Evaluating Educational Programs: the need and the response.* Paris: OECD/CERI.
TAWNEY, D. (ed) (1976) *Curriculum Evaluation Today.* London: Macmillan.
TYLER, R. W. (1949) *Basic Principles of Curriculum Design.* Chicago: University of Chicago Press.
UNITED STATES JOINT COMMITTEE ON STANDARDS FOR EDUCATIONAL EVALUATION (1981) *Standards for the Evaluation of Educational Programs, Projects, and Materials.* New York: McGraw-Hill.

Appendix 1: IEA Studies

INTERNATIONAL REPORTS OF IEA STUDIES

CARROLL, J. B. (1975) *The Teaching of French as a Foreign Language in Eight Countries.* Stockholm: Almqvist & Wiksell/New York: John Wiley.

COMBER, L. C. and KEEVES, J. P. (1973) *Science Education in Nineteen Countries: an empirical study.* Stockholm: Almqvist & Wiksell/New York: John Wiley.

FOSHAY, A. W. (ed) (1962) *Educational Achievements of 13-year-olds in Twelve Countries.* Hamburg: UNESCO Institute for Education.

HUSEN, T. (ed) (1967) *International Study of Achievement in Mathematics: a comparison of twelve countries.* Volumes I and II. Stockholm: Almqvist & Wiksell/New York: John Wiley.

LEWIS, E. G. and MASSAD, C. E. (1975) *The Teaching of English as a Foreign Language in Ten Countries.* Stockholm: Almqvist & Wiksell/New York: John Wiley.

PASSOW, A. H., NOAH, J. J., ECKSTEIN, M. A. and MALLEA, J. R. (1976) *The National Case Study: an empirical comparative study of twenty-one educational systems.* Stockholm: Almqvist & Wiksell/New York: John Wiley

PEAKER, G. F. (1975) *An Empirical Study of Education in Twenty-One Countries: a technical report.* Stockholm: Almqvist & Wiksell/New York: John Wiley.

PURVES, A. C. (1973) *Literature Education in Ten Countries: an empirical study.* Stockholm: Almqvist & Wiksell/New York: John Wiley.

RYAN, D. W. and ANDERSON, L. W. (ed.) (1984) Rethinking research on teaching: lessons learned from an international study, *Evaluation in Education,* 8.

THORNDIKE, R. L. (1973) *Reading Comprehension Education in Fifteen Countries: an empirical study.* Stockholm: Almqvist & Wiksell/New York: John Wiley.

TORNEY, J. V., OPPENHEIM, A. N., and FARNEN, R. F. (1976) *Civic Education in Ten Countries: an empirical study.* Stockholm: Almqvist & Wiksell/New York: John Wiley.

WALKER, D. A. (1976) *The IEA Six Subject Survey: an empirical study of education in twenty-one countries.* Stockholm: Almqvist & Wiksell/New York: John Wiley.

List of Participants
Liste des Participants

I   CHAIRMAN, RAPPORTEUR AND LECTURERS/PRESIDENT, RAPPORTEUR ET CONFERENCIERS

Dr Sally BROWN (Chairperson), Director, Scottish Council for Research in Education (SCRE), 15 St John Street, GB - EDINBURGH EH8 8JR

Prof. John NISBET (Rapporteur General), Head of Department, Department of Education, University of Aberdeen, King's College, GB - ABERDEEN AB9 2UB

Ms Gwynneth DEAKINS, MSC TVEI Unit, 236 Gray's Inn Road, GB - LONDON WC1X 8HL

Mr Harry BLACK, The Scottish Council for Research in Education, 15 St John Street, GB - EDINBURGH EH8 8JR

Mr Mogens JANSEN, The Danish Institute for Educational Research, 28 Hermodsgade, DK - 2200 COPENHAGEN N

Dr Helen SIMONS, Head of Department of Curriculum, Institute of Education, The University of London, 20 Bedford Way, GB - LONDON WC1H 0AL

Mr Lars JOHANSSON, Director of Education, Swedish National Board of Education, Skoloverstyrelsen, -106 42 STOCKHOLM

Mr Andre HUSSENET, Inspecteur General de l'Education Nationale, Ministere de l'Education Nationale, 96 Boulevard Bessieres, F - 75017 PARIS

Mr **Robert LONG,** Senior Adviser, Oxfordshire County Council Education Department, Macclesfield House, New Road, GB - OXFORD OX1 1NA

II *DELEGATES/DELEGUES*

AUSTRIA/AUTRICHE
Univ. Dozent , Dr Friedrich WEYERMULLER, Direktor des Padagogischen Instituts des Landes Tirol, Haymongasse 6a, A-6020 INNSBRUCK

BELGIUM/BELGIQUE
Dr Arno LIBOTTON, Charge de cours a la Faculte de Psychologie et de Pedagogie, de l'Universite Libre de Bruxelles, (Vrije Universiteit van Brussel), Pleinlaan 2, B-1050 BRUSSELS

Monsieur Sylvain COURTOIS, State's Inspector, Racourstraat 83, B-3400 LANDEN

CANADA
Monsieur Alain MERCIER, Direction de la sanction des etudes, 1035, De la Chevrotiere, 10e etage, QUEBEC (QC), G1R 5A5

Mr Art PEDDICORD, Associate Director, Evaluation and Monitoring, Alberta Department of Education, 11160 Jasper Avenue, EDMONTON, Alberta T5K 0L2

Mr Ron CUSSONS, Education Officer, Programme Implementation and Review Branch, Ontario Ministry of Education, Mowat Block - 18th Floor, Queen's Park, 900 Bay Street, TORONTO, Ontario M7A 1L2

DENMARK/DANEMARK
Mr Ib FISCHER HANSEN, General Inspector of Education, Directorate for Upper Secondary Education, Amagertorv 10, DK - 1160 COPENHAGEN K

FRANCE
Madame Martine LE GUEN, Chef du Bureau de l'evaluation pedagogique dans les lycees et colleges a la Direction de l'evaluation, Ministere de l'Education Nationale, Direction de l'Evaluation et de la Prospective, 142, rue du Bac, F-75007 PARIS

FEDERAL REPUBLIC OF GERMANY/REPUBLIQUE FEDERALE D'ALLEMAGNE
Professor Dr. Karlheinz INGENKAMP, Erziehungswissenschaftliche Hochschule, Rheinland-Pfalz, Abteilung Landau, Im Fort 7, D - 6740 LANDAU/PFALZ

Prof. Dr. Heinrich WOTTAWA, Ruhruniversitat Bochum, Universitatsstrasse 150, D-4630 BOCHUM3

GREECE/GRECE
Professor Christos FRANGOS, President of the Department of Education at the University of Thessaloniki, Director of the EDURIT, THESSALONIKI, GR - GREECE

ICELAND/ISLANDE
Professor Sigridur VALGEIRSDOTTIR, Director of the Institute of Educational Research, V/Laufasveg (Kennaraskolahusid), ISL - 101 REYKJAVIK

IRELAND/IRLANDE
Excused/excuse

ITALY/ITALIE
Excused/excuse

LUXEMBOURG
Professeur MARIE-PAULE MAURER, Institut superieur d'etudes et de recherches pedagogiques, Boite postale 2, L-7201 WALFERDANGE

NETHERLAND/PAYS BAS
DR W HOEBEN, Institute for Educational Research (RION), PO Box 1286, NL-9701 BG GRONINGEN

Ms Dr. L VAN TILBORG, Institute for Educational Research (SVO), Sweelinckplein 14, NL-2517 GK DEN HAAG

NORWAY/NORVEGE
Professor Tom TILLER, Krognesvejen 5B, N - 9000 TROMSO

Mr Ole BRISEID, Head of Division, Department of Upper Secondary Education, Ministry of Church and Education, PO Box 8119 Dep., N - 0032 OSLO 1

Mr Peder HAUG, Research Worker, Moreforsking, Postbox 325, N-6101 VOLDA

PORTUGAL
Madame Maria DO CARMO CLIMACO, Directora de Servicos de Estudos, Gabinete de Estudos e Planeamento, Ministerio da Educacao, Av. Miguel Bombarda 20, 5, P-1093 LISBOA CODEX

SPAIN/ESPAGNE
Excuse/excuse

SWEDEN/SUEDE
Mr Esse LOVGREN, Director of Education, Head of Department, National Board of Education (Skoloverstyrelsen), S-106 40 STOCKHOLM

UNITED KINGDOM/ROYAUME-UNI
Dr Seamus HEGARTY, National Foundation for Research in England and Wales (NFER), The Mere, Upton Park, GB - SLOUGH, Berskhire SL1 2DQ

OTHER PARTICIPANTS FROM THE UNITED KINGDOM/ AUTRES PARTICIPANTS DU ROYAUME-UNI

SCOTTISH EDUCATION DEPARTMENT (SED)
Mrs Judith DUNCAN, Scottish Education Department, Room 4/39, New St Andrew's House, GB - EDINBURGH EH1 3SY

Mrs Hope JOHNSTON, Scottish Education Department, Room 4/38 New St Andrew's House, GB - EDINBURGH EH1 3SY

Mr A McGLYNN, HMCI, Scottish Education Department, New St Andrew's House, GB - EDINBURGH EH1 3SY

Mr Brian SEMPLE, Scottish Education Department, New St Andrew's House, GB - EDINBURGH EH1 3SY

SCOTTISH COUNCIL FOR RESEARCH IN EDUCATION (SCRE)
Mr David BUTTS, 15 Randolph Road, GB - STIRLING FK8 2AW

Mrs Marion DEVINE, Scottish Council for Research in Education, 15 St John Street, GB - EDINBURGH EH8 8JR

Mrs Heather MALCOLM, Scottish Council for Research in Education, 15 St John Street, GB - EDINBURGH EH8 8JR

Ms Candy MacDONALD, Scottish Council for Research in Education, 15 St John Street, GB - EDINBURGH EH8 8JR

Mrs Pamela MUNN, Scottish Council for Research in Education, 15 St John Street, GB - EDINBURGH EH8 8JR

Ms Rosemary WAKE, Scottish Council for Research in Education, 15 St John Street, GB - EDINBURGH EH8 8JR

SCOTTISH CONSULTATIVE COUNCIL ON THE CURRICULUM (SCCC)
Mr Ian BARR, Director, Curriculum Development and Evaluation, Scottish Consultative Council on the Curriculum, Lymehurst House, 76 Southbrae Drive, GB - GLASGOW G13 1PP

Sister Maire GALLAGHER, Chairman, Scottish Consultative Council on the Curriculum, Convent of Notre Dame, Cardross Road, GB - DUMBARTON G82 4DH

Mr David McNICOLL, Chief Executive, Scottish Consultative Council on the Curriculum, 17 St John Street, GB - EDINBURGH EH8 8DG

Mr David G ROBERTSON, Director of Education, Tayside Regional Council, 28 Crichton Strett, GB - DUNDEE DD1 3RJ

Mr Sydney SMYTH, Scottish Consultative Council on the Curriculum, 17 St John Street, GB - EDINBURGH EH8 8DG

Mr Dan TAYLOR, Scottish Consultative Council on the Curriculum, Kirkhillhead, Walker's Crescent, Lhanbryde, GB - ELGIN IV30 3PB

UNIVERSITIES
Dr W Bryan DOCKRELL, The Coach House, Carberry Road, Inveresk, MUSSELBURGH. EH21 7TN

Mr Richard LANEC, Education Officer, University of Bristol, School of Education, 35 Berkeley Square, GB - BRISTOL BS8 1JA

Mr M MERSON, Department of Education, University of Warwick, Westwood, GB - COVENTRY CV4 7AL

Dr Joyce WATT, Department of Education, University of Aberdeen, King's College, GB - ABERDEEN AB9 2UB

COLLEGES
Mr Brian ARNOLD, Northern College of Education, (Aberdeen Campus), Hilton Place, GB - ABERDEEN AB9 1FA

Dr James KIDD, Department of Teaching Studies, Moray House College of Education, Holyrood Road, GB - EDINBURGH EH8 8AQ

Mr Gordon KIRK, Principal, Moray House College of Education, Holyrood Road, GB - EDINBURGH EH8 8AQ

Ms J McCLOSKY, Special Educational Needs, St Andrew's College of Education, Duntocher Road, Bearsden, GB - GLASGOW.

Mr A Douglas WEIR, Director of Research (Jordanhill College), 23 Dumyat Drive, GB - FALKIRK FK1 5PA

OTHERS
Ms M PIRIE, Department of Employment (Training Agency), 12 Oak Grove, Pitcorthie, GB- DUNFERMLINE, Fife

Dr John RAVEN, Consultant, 30 Great King Street, GB-EDINBURGH

Mr Neil TOPPIN, Strathclyde Regional Council, 20 India Street, GB - GLASGOW

Ms Penelope WESTON, Project Leader, National Foundation for Educational Research in England and Wales (NFER), The Mere, Upton Park, GB - SLOUGH SL1 2DQ

III OBSERVERS/OBSERVATEURS
- UNESCO

- OECD/OCDE

- COMMISSION OF THE EUROPEAN COMMUNITIES/ COMMISSION DES COMMUNAUTES EUROPEENNES
  Excused/excuse

NORDIC COUNCIL
Mr Tore KARLSSON, The Secretariat of the Nordic Council of Ministers, Store Strandstraede 18, DK-1255 COPENHAGEN K

WORLD CONFEDERATION OF ORGANISATIONS OF THE TEACHING PROFESSION (WCOTP)/CONFEDERATION MONDIALE DES ORGANISATIONS DE LA PROFESSION ENSEIGNANTE (CMOPE)
Mr Marc-Alain BERBERAT, Secretaire General Adjoint, WCOTP/CMOPE, 5 avenue du Moulin, CH-1110 MORGES

WORLD FEDERATION OF TEACHERS' UNIONS/FEDERATION INTERNATIONALE SYNDICALE DE L'ENSEIGNEMENT (FISE)

ASSOCIATION FOR TEACHER EDUCATION IN EUROPE (ATEE)/ASSOCIATION POUR LA FORMATION DES ENSEIGNANTS EN EUROPE

INSTITUT EUROPEEN D'EDUCATION ET DE POLITIQUE SOCIALE

INTERNATIONAL ASSOCIATION FOR THE EVALUATION OF EDUCATIONAL ACHIEVEMENT (IEA)
Excused/excuse

IV   ORGANISERS/ORGANISATEURS
1.   *SCOTTISH COUNCIL FOR RESEARCH IN EDUCATION*

Dr Sally BROWN, Director, Scottish Council for Research in Education (SCRE), 15 St John Street, GB - EDINBURGH EH8 8JR

SUPPORT STAFF
Mr David GILHOOLY, Administrative Officer, SCRE

Mrs Hedda KING, Secretary, SCRE

Mrs Moira SIMPSON, Cashier, SCRE

Mrs May YOUNG, Secretary, SCRE

2. *COUNCIL OF EUROPE/CONSEIL DE L'EUROPE*
   Dr Michael VORBECK, Head of the Section for Educational Research and Documentation, BP 431 R6, F-67006 STRASBOURG CEDEX

   Mme Daniele IMBERT, Secretary

   INTERPRETERS/INTERPRETES
   Madame Eline AITKEN-GONDOIN, 27 rue Gagarine, F-59139 WATTIGNIES

   Madame Huong DO, 5 Passage Bullourde, F-75011 PARIS

NEW

School Effectiveness and School Improvement

Editors
Bert Creemers, University of Groningen, the Netherlands
Ton Peters, University of Rotterdam, the Netherlands
Dave Reynolds, University of Wales College of Cardiff, U.K.

This volume contains a selection of the papers which were given at the Second International Congress for School Effectiveness, the Netherlands, January 1989.
Section 1 contains the papers related to the concerns of school effectiveness and improvement.
Section 2 contains reports on the 'state of the art" for effectiveness and improvement in different countries.
Section 3 presents a wide variety of research, much of it very recent, into the factors within schools that are associated with "effectiveness" and the consistency of findings over time and across contexts and countries.
Section 4 moves on from research to practice by looking at improvement programmes at school and school district level, together with material on the educational policy arrangements for "improvement" that exists within some cultures.
Section 5 consists of reflections on what has been accomplished and what remains to be accomplished in the next decade. This book offers a wide, up-to-date range of theoretical and practical aspects of school effectiveness across the world.

In USA and Canada, mail your order to:

Taylor & Francis Inc.
1900 Frost Road, Suite 101
BRISTOL, PA 19007, USA
Telephone 1-800-821-8312 (toll-free)
Fax 215-785-5515

School Effectiveness and School Improvement
Creemers/Peters/Reynolds
ISBN 90 265 1008 X
Dgl. 72.50, 396 pp.

Available through your bookseller

SWETS & ZEITLINGER B.V.
Publishing Service
P.O. Box 825, 2160 SZ LISSE HOLLAND, Fax 31 2521-15888

Paul Vedder (Ed.)

Fundamental Studies in Educational Research

In this volume eight scholars – Walberg, Windham, Clifford, Weinert, Siguan, Cummins, Entwistle and Purves – present problems in their particular domain of expertise which, in their view, should be subjected to fundamental educational research. The focus is on topics such as school effectiveness, multicultural and multilingual education, motivation and differentiation strategies and learner differences. Notwithstanding the wide diversity of the research ideas that are put forward, the contributions are unanimous in their strong plea for fundamental educational research. Fundamental research can never be short-term research and should be conducted and evaluated relatively independently from the everchanging wishes for research of educational policy makers.

The book leaves no doubt that concern for improving school practice is by no means out of place when one addresses fundamental issues in educational research. On the contrary, the eventual improvement of school practice is viewed as a major motive for conducting fundamental educational research in the first place.

1990, 224 pp., ISBN 90 265 1057 8, hardbound.

In the USA and Canada available from:
Taylor & Francis Inc. International Publishers
1900 Frost Road, Suite 101
Bristol, PA 19007, USA
Telephone (215) 785 5800

Also available from your bookseller.

SWETS & ZEITLINGER B.V.　　　　　　　　　　　　PUBLISHERS
PUBLISHING SERVICE

Heereweg 347, 2161 CA, Lisse, The Netherlands, Telephone 02521-35111